ARGENT
VISUAL G
CLARIN

BUENOS AIRES
Mini-tourism

Approved by the Secretaría de Turismo y Deporte.

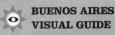

BUENOS AIRES
VISUAL GUIDE
Mini-tourism

ClarínX viajes

SUMMARY

BUENOS AIRES
VISUAL GUIDE
Mini-tourism

Is a special project executed by Clarín

PRESIDENT
EDITORIAL DIRECTOR
Ernestina Herrera de Noble

PROJECT EXECUTION
Roberto Fernández Taboada
Norberto Angeletti

EDITORIAL COORDINATION
Fernando Muñoz Pace
Pablo Ravaschino

HISTORICAL ADVISER
Eliana de Arrascaeta

GENERAL EDITING
Aurelio Valdearena
Alejandra Sayago
Estela Arias

ITINERARY EDITING
Julián Chappa
Lidia Cepeda
Fernando Arauz
Gedalio Tarasow

PHOTOGRAPHIC SERVICES
Archivo Clarín
Archivo Ignacio Corbalán
Archivo General de la Nación
Roberto Rainer Cinti
Lucio Contigiani
Hernán Goñi
Saturnino Herrero Mitjans
Museo de la Casa de Gobierno
Carlos Alberto Passera

PHOTOCHROMISM
Artes Gráficas Rioplatense S.A.

PRINTING AND BINDING
I. Gráficas Mármol S.L.

First Edition, January, 2002.
Argentina Visual Guides Clarín
ISBN 950-782-165-1
Buenos Aires Visual Guide mini-tourism
ISBN 950-782-228-3
Clarín A.G.E.A. S. A. 2001.
All rights reserved.
Duty copy B-21.739-2002
Neither the complete publication nor part of
this book may be reproduced in any form or by
any electronic or mechanical means, including
information storage and retrieval systems
without permission in writing from the
publisher Clarín newspaper.
Notwithstanding the revision done to the work,
the editor is no responsible for mistakes or omis-
sions in this guide because changes in timetables,
addresses and services may occur. It is advisable
to call the published telephones before visiting
the sites to check visiting days and hours.
For comments and suggestions via Internet:
guiasturclarin@agea.com.ar, Mailing address:
Clarín Proyectos Especiales. 1872, Tacuarí Street.
Buenos Aires, Argentina.Zip Code 1140.
Assistance to the Reader: (54-11) 4510 4545
Cartography is in accordance with the
regulations established by the Executive Power
by IGM Docket GG1 2643/5.

**GENERAL DESIGN
AND EXECUTION**
Editorial Sol 90 S.L.

EDITORIAL DIRECTOR
Osvaldo Leboso

ART DIRECTOR
Fabián Cassan

PUBLISHER
Marc Llorens

ENGLISH TRANSLATOR
Rosa Vita

EDITORIAL BOARD
Ramiro Espiño
Nicolás Kugler
Ricardo Marín
María José Solís

LAYOUT
Agustina Arguijo
Sergi Ibañez
Lorena Marchetti
Paula Seré
Carolina Tirelli Carri

**PRODUCTION
AND COORDINATION
OF ILLUSTRATIONS**
Andrea Giacobone

**THREE-DIMENSIONAL
ILLUSTRATIONS**
Isidro López
Marcel Socías
Estudio de Arquitectura
Tófalo-Niro

**COMPUTARIZED GRAPHICS
AND CARTOGRAPHY**
Aldo Chiappe
Ana Gueller
Jorge Portaz

PHOTOGRAPHS
Juan Siquot
Julio Giustozzi

TOURIST ADVISER
Federico Kirbus

DOCUMENTALIST
Natalia Kovacic

ARCHIVAL PHOTOGRAPHS
Mariela Petrocelli

PRODUCER
Marta Kordon

*Our special thanks to
Secretaría de Turismo y
Deporte for their advice and
logistical support during the
creation of this guidebook.*

Aerial view of Martín García island.

Ranch house on estancia Santa Rita.

Local bar on the La Cinacina ranch.

3

Museo del Muñeco (Doll Museum).

Three-dimensional
drawing of the
Tigre delta area.

How to Use This Guidebook

This guide is divided into three parts. GENERAL INFORMATION explains some of the history, geography and customs of Buenos Aires and the surrounding area. The ITINERARIES are our suggested routes, divided into sectors, which include maps and three-dimensional pictures of buildings and outstanding natural areas. Finally, the SERVICES section contains indispensable information for the traveler about transport, accommodation, gastronomy, leisure activities and shopping.

❶ GENERAL INFORMATION.
This first part is divided into three sections: the history of the city and the region, general geography and a section on customs, concerning past and present habits. *Example on page 14.*

Basílica de Luján

Luján Basilica. The most important of Roman Catholic Church in Argentina, is an imposing new Gothic style church located in Plaza Belgrano in Luján. Each year in May and October, millions of pilgrims come from all America.

THE MAIN ALTAR, donated by Armstrong family at the beginning of 20° Century is made of marble, bronze and gold. Eight million people have visited the niche with the Virgin behind the altar.

IN A CRYPT on the basement these are several images of Virgin Mary worshipped in different countries of the world.

THE TWO ORGANS are both valuable European instruments, the largest has 5,000 pipes

GOTHIC STYLE, Fathers Salvaire and Archbishop Anneiros had the ideas of erecting a church inspired in French cathedrals ...

❷ GENERAL ITINERARIES MAP. The second part of the guide begins with a general map of all of the itineraries, and which also shows the main communication routes that connect up each of these itineraries. *Example on page 20.*

Between the River and La Pampa

❸ THREE-DIMENSIONAL MAPS.
The itinerary is divided into sectors and shown on the map. Each sector is enlarged on another detailed three-dimensional map, where the places of interest are identified by a reference number which is used in the pages that follow. *Examples on pages 24 and 26.*

From San Isidro to Isla Martín García

❹ THREE-DIMENSIONAL PICTURES.

The main buildings and natural areas in each sector are shown in detailed three-dimensional pictures. *Example on page 58.*

ESCOBAR TO SAN ANDRES DE GILES | SAN ANTONIO DE ARECO AND SURROUNDINGS

USEFUL INFORMATION
ADDRESS: 51 San Martin St. Ph. 02323 42–1070.
HOURS: The basilica is open every day from 7 AM to 8 PM. The historical exhibition is open Tuesday to Sunday from 10 AM to 12 PM and 2 PM to 6 PM.
GUIDED TOURS: To have information about regular guided tours and educational tours, the visitor should contact telephone (02323) 43–5101.

POPE JOHN PAUL II VISIT
The pope celebrated a mass in front of the Luján Basilica for 800 thousand people on June 11, 1982.

THE STAINED GLASS works from 19th Century constitute one of the largest collections in Argentina.

THE MAIN NAVE is 97 m (318 ft) in length and 30 m (98 ft) in height.

THE PRIESTS' DWELLINGS are located in the interior garden area.

THE MUSEUM exhibits a replica of the Luján Virgin wearing the original mantle with a escutcheon from 1900.

THE VIRGIN'S CROWN containing 365 precious stones was blessed by Pope Leon XIII.

THE EXHIBITION displays the historical and religious evolution of Luján including Father Salvaire history. The distinction granted by Pope John Paul II during his visit is exhibited between a gold tabernacle and precious stones.

❺ SERVICES.

The third part of the guide deals with tourist services, and is comprised of the following sections: basic information, transport, accommodation, restaurants, leisure and shopping. *Example on page 124.*

GENERAL REFERENCES

◆) CONNECTION OF THE INFORMATION

III USEFUL INFORMATION

○ LINK WITH OTHER PAGE

► LINK WITH A POINT OF INTEREST

SPECIAL AREAS

🏛 HISTORICAL MONUMENT

🏵 MANKIND PATRIMONY

🏞 NATIONAL PARK

🐚 BIOSPHERE RESERVE

NOTICES

🏠 HABITS

🏃 SPORTS

📷 OBSERVATORY

🐾 FAUNA

🌿 FLORA

👁 CONSIDERATIONS

🚗 BY CAR

RANKING OF THE SIGHTS

✶✶✶✶ Impossible to miss
✶✶✶ Excellent
✶✶ Very Good
✶ Very Interesting

This grading system is used on the itinerary maps and sector maps.

MAPS GLOSSARY

Avenue	*Avenida*
Marshland	*Bañado*
Forest	*Bosque*
Street	*Calle*
Canal	*Canal*
Road	*Camino*
Delta	*Delta*
Dike	*Dique*
Island	*Isla*
Small lake	*Laguna*
Beach	*Playa*
Square	*Plaza*
Point	*Punta*
River	*Río*

GAUCHOS IN SAN ANTONIO DE ARECO

RIVER FERRY ON THE LUJAN RIVER

AERIAL VIEW OF ISLA MARTIN GARCIA

LOCAL LIBRARY, SAN ISIDRO

BIBLIOTECA POPULA

TEATRO ARGENTINO, LA PLATA

MUSEO CIENCIAS NATURALES, LA PLATA

FISHERMEN AT THE PORT OF TIGRE

HISTORIC PHOTOGRAPH, SAN ISIDRO RACETRACK

JAPANESE GARDEN, ESCOBAR

GENERAL INFORMATION

Tradition and Modernity

Many of the events which marked Argentine history took place in the Buenos Aires area. The city's identity is based on a rural culture, with the Gaucho as protagonist of the agricultural-cattle-raising tradition, which has been the driving force behind the country's economic development. In the 21st Century, the remains of this heritage have combined with a new society which is modern and developed and faithful to its past.

EL OMBU RANCH

SUMMARY

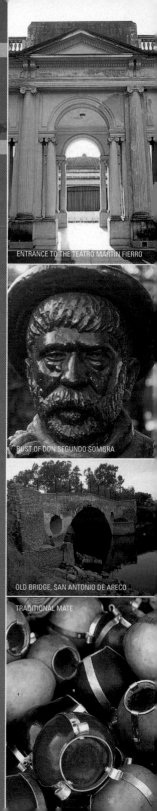

ENTRANCE TO THE TEATRO MARTIN FIERRO

BUST OF DON SEGUNDO SOMBRA

OLD BRIDGE, SAN ANTONIO DE ARECO

TRADITIONAL MATE

From the City's Origins to the Modern Day

Since the discovery of Río de la Plata and the introduction of the Viceroyship, the region's development has been linked to territorial expansion into Indian land and the consolidation of the agricultural and cattle-raising economy. The arrival of the railway in the 19th Century gave a new impetus to Buenos Aires.

INDIGENOUS POPULATION. When the Conquistadors arrived, the west bank of Río de La Plata, and part of what is now Buenos Aires province, was inhabited by the Querandi people, who were nomads, hunter-gatherers and fishermen. Meanwhile, Guarani tribes lived out on the Río Paraná delta.

Querandi Indian

Magellan   Cabot

Solís' signature

THE FIRST EXPLORERS. Juan Díaz de Solís (1516), Ferdinand Magellan (1519) and Sebastian Cabot (1525) all sailed up Río de la Plata looking for a route through to the Pacific.

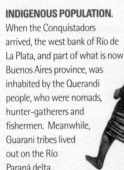

CREATION OF THE VICEROYSHIP. In 1776, the Viceroyship of Río de La Plata was established, with jurisdiction over the northern part of what is now Buenos Aires province, La Banda Oriental (Eastern strip), Paraguay, Tucumán, Cuyo and Upper Peru. Pedro de Cevallos *(see photo)* was nominated temporary Viceroy.

Caracas

Guayaquil

Lima

PORTUGUESE TERRITORY

RIO DE LA PLATA VICEROYSHIP

Potosí

Asunción

Buenos Aires

CHILEAN GENERAL CAPTAINCY

FORTS AND SALT FLATS. In 1718, small forts were built at Chascomús, Lobos, Areco and Luján to strengthen the frontier with Indian territory. On the initiative of the Viceroy Vertiz, these settlements grew thanks to the salt flats and the dairies *(engravings)*.

1833

Lithograph of the 1833 Desert Campaign.

PUSHING BACK THE FRONTIERS

In 1827-1828, Juan Manuel de Rosas built forts to strengthen the provincial borders in the Luján area, and in 1833 he led a successful campaign against the Indians which established new frontiers and encouraged the development of settlements in Buenos Aires province, which until then had been in a state of siege.

ARGENTINE CONFEDERATION

STATE OF BUENOS AIRES

THE SECESSION. In 1853, the government of Buenos Aires rejected the Congreso General Constituyente imposed by Justo José de Urquiza *(center)*. Valentín Alsina *(left)* and Bartolomé Mitre *(right)* were the leaders of the independence movement. In 1854, Buenos Aires seceded from the provinces, creating a territory *(see map)* which included all of the towns within its area.

THE DRIVING FORCE OF COMMERCE

Thanks to wool, lamb and beef exports, the income for Buenos Aires and its surrounding area in 1855 doubled that of the rest of the Confederation. Towns in Buenos Aires province such as San Antonio de Areco, Chascomús, Lobos and Luján produced much of these goods, which were shipped off to the most important ports in the world.

THE ARRIVAL OF THE RAILWAY.

The railway system grew rapidly from 1860 onwards, connecting agricultural areas with the port of Buenos Aires. In 1864, the Ferrocarril del Sur (Southern Railway) joined the city to Chascomús, while in 1876 the Tigre line was opened. Most of the locomotives were imported from England *(see photos)*.

The Identity of the New Century

From the end of the 19th Century onwards, the towns around Buenos Aires witnessed historical events which changed the region forever, events such as the founding of a new provincial capital (La Plata), Tigre's growth as an aristocratic town, the drift of the rural population into the city and, finally, the arrival of international culture.

LA PLATA

When Buenos Aires was nominated Federal Capital, a new Provincial capital was created, and on November 19, 1882, Dardo Rocha founded La Plata.

DARDO ROCHA

Born in Buenos Aires in 1938, Dardo Rocha was a lawyer, a journalist and a soldier who became the force behind the founding of La Plata. On May 1st, 1881, he took over as Governor of the Buenos Aires province, from where he organized the creation of the new capital. He fought under Mitre in the battles of Cepeda and Pavón.

CITY OF DIAGONAL LINES

Pedro Benoit, engineer and photographer, designed the layout for the city of La Plata, which was built on Las Lomas de la Ensenada, on the initiative of the Governor Dardo Rocha. He also constructed the city's most important public buildings.

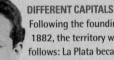

DIFFERENT CAPITALS

Following the founding of La Plata in 1882, the territory was organized as follows: La Plata became the capital of Buenos Aires province, while the city of Buenos Aires became the capital of the Republic and the seat of the national government.

IMMIGRANTS. The flow of immigrants reached a peak in 1870, with an influx of almost **40,000** people. Though most of them remained in the capital and the immediate environs, many of them went to live in towns in the province, where they worked in agriculture.

CREATION OF THE BASILICA OF LUJAN

On May 15, 1887, the foundation stone of the Basílica of Luján was given its ritual blessing. Construction was completed in 1930. Padre Jorge Salvaire was the driving force behind the creation of the largest Christian temple in Argentina, though it was completed under the French architect Ulderico Courtois.

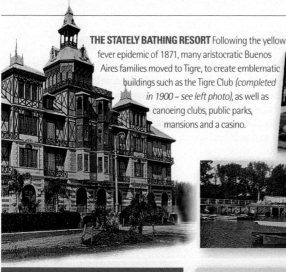

THE STATELY BATHING RESORT Following the yellow fever epidemic of 1871, many aristocratic Buenos Aires families moved to Tigre, to create emblematic buildings such as the Tigre Club *(completed in 1900 – see left photo)*, as well as canoeing clubs, public parks, mansions and a casino.

1940

The petrochemical industry on the banks of the Riachuelo.

CULTURE AT VILLA OCAMPO
Located in San Isidro, this was a meeting place for many of the most important artists and intellectuals of the 20th Century. Between the 1920s and the 1960s, luminaries such as Borges, Bioy Casares, Albert Camus, Graham Greene, Igor Stravinsky, André Malraux and Le Corbusier spent time here.

FROM THE COUNTRY TO THE CITY
In around 1940 a large industrial belt began to grow around the Federal Capital. This process of urban growth was boosted by the influx of the population from the interior of the country and from towns in Buenos Aires province. As a result, many of these towns became greatly de-populated.

THE PRISON ISLAND
In 1765, Isla Martín García became a prison island, and some of its most famous "guests" were the presidents Hipólito Yrigoyen, Juan Domingo Perón and Arturo Frondizi *(see photo)*, all in the 20th Century.

THE NEW FACE OF THE RIVER
Following years of decline and disrepair, the northern part of the shore of Río de la Plata and the Tigre delta were dramatically renovated. The restoration of the Tren de la Costa line *(see photo)*, the creation of theme parks and leisure centers and investment into infrastructure all helped the area to regain its former splendor and beauty.

Between the Delta and the Plain

Near Buenos Aires, interesting natural formations are found. One of them is the Paraná Delta with lush vegetation and animal life, some species are typical of forests. The other is the pasture of the Pampa plains. There, in the estancias take place one of the main activities of the Buenos Aires province economy: cattle raising and grain farming. There are also the Pampa lakes for fishing and nautical sports.

DELTA DRAWING

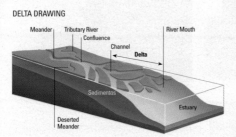

THE PARANA DELTA is originated in the amassing of sediment, mainly sand, mud and clay at the confluence of Rio de la Plata and Paraná rivers. When the two rivers carrying different masses of water meet, the Paraná current velocity decreases and favors the deposit of sediments making up the isles.

PARANA VEGETATION

The Paraná river drags a big amount of seeds gathered along its route. Some of them grow in the Delta soil originating a forest in the shore. From these seeds grow the ceiba tree which bears the Argentine national flower, the ceibo (*photo*).

IT IS A TERRITORY IN EXPANSION. Paraná Delta moves forward to Buenos Aires direction with an average of 46.5 meters per year. If the movement continues steadily, in 2236 it will reach Nuñez neighborhood in Federal Capital. In 2580 the isles will be opposite the Riachuelo mouth.

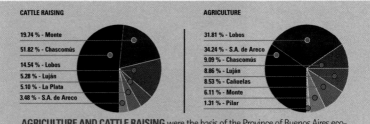

CATTLE RAISING

- 19.74 % - Monte
- 51.82 % - Chascomús
- 14.54 % - Lobos
- 5.28 % - Luján
- 5.10 % - La Plata
- 3.48 % - S.A. de Areco

AGRICULTURE

- 31.81 % - Lobos
- 34.24 % - S.A. de Areco
- 9.09 % - Chascomús
- 8.86 % - Luján
- 8.53 % - Cañuelas
- 6.11 % - Monte
- 1.31 % - Pilar

AGRICULTURE AND CATTLE RAISING were the basis of the Province of Buenos Aires economic development. San Antonio de Areco and Chascomús are remarkable for their production.

SOURCE: INDEC BUENOS AIRES PROVINCIAL CATTLE TRADE DEPARTMENT

PAMPA LAKES VEGETATION

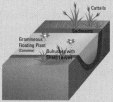

A sunken ground collecting water permanently.

Sediments contribute to the vegetation nourishment.

LAGOONS. The lagoons in Buenos Aires province are surfaces of fresh or salty waters with well-defined edges. The environment conditions where water and nutrients are plenty favor the growing of different kind of vegetation. La Pampa lagoons are abundant in plants with flowers including the saeta and the marshy land daisies that are very common. However, the most characteristic are bulrushes growing at the shores. There are also white peach trees with their purple flowers and black fruit usually growing in shallow waters. Duckweed and fern form floating plants at the shore.

BUENOS AIRES PAMPA

Pampean soil is rich in humus favoring the growing of pasture and few trees.

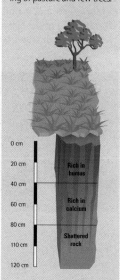

0 cm

20 cm — Rich in humus

40 cm

60 cm — Rich in calcium

80 cm

110 cm — Shattered rock

120 cm

15

RURAL FAUNA

Pampean venison, American ostrich, viscacha, *mulitas*, woodpecker and American sparrow hawk live together with the cattle raised in the area *estancias*. Even though this species are predominant, some of them are threatened with extinction.

American Ostrich.

Viscacha.

Mulitas.

Rural Woodpecker.

American Sparrow Hawk .

Pampean Venison.

Rural Influences

Everyday life in towns around Buenos Aires is filled with customs that are typical of rural Creole culture: Gaucho traditions, religious celebrations and a rich imaginative world which many of the greatest Argentinian writers have drawn on through the ages.

Tigre

Strolling along the canals at Tigre is a popular pastime for people living in areas around the city. The beautiful summer bathing resorts and the marvelous Puerto de Frutos *(left photo)* make this one of the most important leisure areas.

LIVING FOLKLORE
The Zamba, the Gato and the Malambo are just some of the typical dances which are still popular today.

Luján

In May and October there are massive pilgrimages to the Basílica of Luján, an event which is of great religious importance to the people of Buenos Aires. Millions of people

from all over Argentina and other neighboring countries walk the traditional paths to the sanctuary of the Virgin of Luján *(left photo)*. The Basílica is the most important Catholic church in Argentina.

Gaucho arts and traditions are still very much alive in many towns, such as San Antonio de Areco, Cañuelas and San Andrés de Giles. These towns often hold competitions and exhibitions of horse-breaking, riding, track races *(right photo)* and stabling. These events are particularly spectacular on national festival days.

The Gaucho

The language
The country people's way of speaking includes many old words and expressions.

CHINA - WOMAN

FACA - KNIFE

PELUDO - DRUNK

THE MATE RITUAL

In Tigre market many typical zucchini matés are on sale (see photo). They can be made by mixing drops of ginger essence, orange peel, cedron leaves and even with cow's milk.

The rural tradition, the magic of Tigre and the city of La Plata have been the inspiration for many of the greatest Argentinian writers.

Güiraldes

Educated in France, he lived in San Antonio de Areco. He succeeded in incorporating Gaucho themes into "serious" literary forms. His book *Don Segundo Sombra* (1926) is a vivid portrait of rural Argentina at the beginning of 20th Century.

17

Lugones

The man who wrote *La Guerra Gaucha* (1905) and *Historia de Sarmiento* (1911), and who won the 1926 National Prize for literature ended his life on an island in Tigre on February 18, 1938.

Conti

One of his most emblematic works, *Sudeste* (1962), takes place in Tigre and depicts the lives of people of the delta, where Haroldo Conti lived for several years.

Bioy Casares

The action of one of his last novels, *La aventura de un fotógrafo en La Plata* (1985), revolves around the capital of Buenos Aires province. Amidst a tangled plot, the author paints a marvelous portrait of the "City of diagonal lines".

José Hernández

"Brothers must be united
Because that is the primary law:
that they be truly united at all times.
Because if they start to fight
amongst each other,
Outsiders will come and devour them."

(*Martín Fierro*, José Hernández)

PINGO – HORSE

PULPERIA – BAR

LLORONAS – SPURS

INFIEL – INDIAN

REPUBLICA DE LOS NIÑOS

HOUSE IN DELTA DEL TIGRE

PULPERIA DE LA ESTANCIA LA CINACINA

HORSES OF THE ESTANCIA LA PORTEÑA

LOBOS LAGOON

HOUSE IN ISLA MARTIN GARCIA

ISLA MARTIN GARCIA

CATEDRAL DE LA PLATA

LA PLATA CATHEDRAL

BUENOS AIRES SURROUNDINGS

Around Nature

In the proximity of Buenos Aires, there is a different world away from the frantic pace of the huge metropolis and the visitor may have different possibilities to tour outside the city. In the north, the Delta del Tigre, in the west the Pampa plains and its traditions, in the south La Plata modern and peaceful city. This semicircular belt with its natural wealth is a good option for those who want new sensations.

SUMMARY

MUSEO RICARDO GUIRALDES

CHASCOMUS LAGOON

MUSEO PAMPEANO DE CHASCOMUS

LEGISLATURA DE LA PLATA

CHASCOMUS TRAIN STATION

Between the River and La Pampa

Four itineraries travel through Buenos Aires outskirts. First, a part of the Río de la Plata coast containing San Isidro city, the Delta del Tigre and Isla Martín García. The second sector is a portion of the Pampean plains and the surrounding areas of San Andrés de Giles and San Antonio de Areco. The third one includes the region of linked lagoons of Lobos, Monte, Chascomús. Lastly, the city of La Plata and the neighboring area.

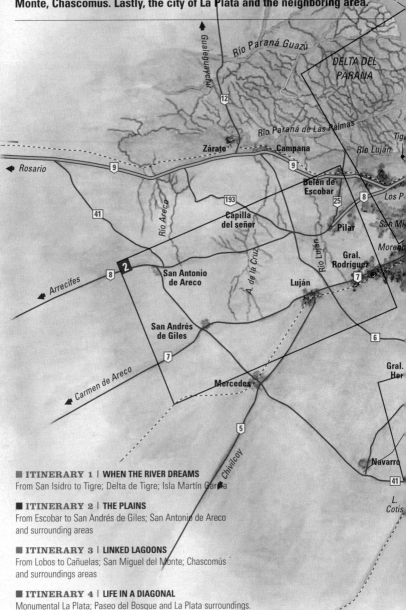

■ **ITINERARY 1** | **WHEN THE RIVER DREAMS**
From San Isidro to Tigre; Delta de Tigre; Isla Martín García

■ **ITINERARY 2** | **THE PLAINS**
From Escobar to San Andrés de Giles; San Antonio de Areco and surrounding areas

■ **ITINERARY 3** | **LINKED LAGOONS**
From Lobos to Cañuelas; San Miguel del Monte; Chascomús and surroundings areas

■ **ITINERARY 4** | **LIFE IN A DIAGONAL**
Monumental La Plata; Paseo del Bosque and La Plata surroundings.

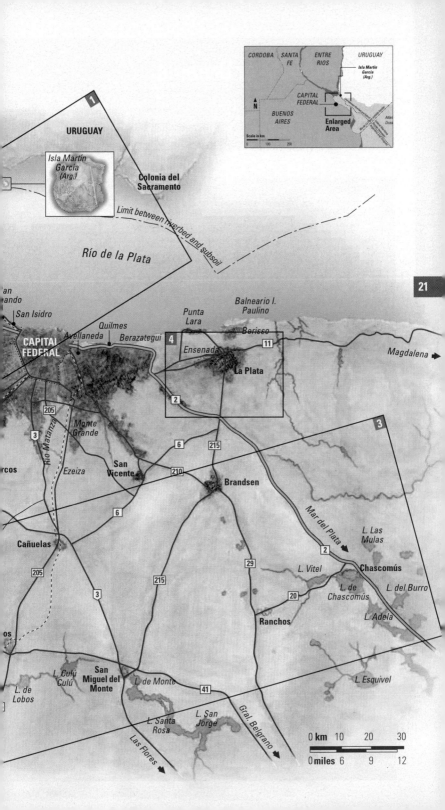

When the River Dreams

The river is the protagonist. Along the coast towards the north is the traditional San Isidro and the picturesque Tigre; further along the river turns into one thousand isles in the delta; in the middle is Martín García with many years of history.

RECREO BANCO PROVINCIA

RÍO DE LA PLATA BINATIONAL COMMISSION

CATEDRAL DE SAN ISIDRO

MARSHMALLOW FLOWER, TYPICAL OF TIGRE

SARMIENTO MUSEUM AND HOUSE

PARQUE DE LA COSTA

LABYRINTH ON ISLA MARTIN GARCIA

COLEGIO SAN JUAN PRECURSOR

TANGERINES FROM THE DELTA

WICKERWORK IN TIGRE

ISLA MARTIN GARCIA

From San Isidro to Isla Martín García

The itinerary by the Delta del Paraná and its surroundings travels through the north part of Gran Buenos Aires, encircled by three rivers. The first sector covers the large urban centers, San Isidro and Tigre with abundant gardens and parks. The second goes to Tigre port where boats sail to travel through the Delta isles with hostels and recreational areas in the shores. The third sector focuses in Isla Martín García, with a unspoiled ecosystem and a colonial past.

Sector 2
DELTA DE TIGRE

SIGHTS TO SEE

❶ Río Luján ✱✱: Centro Náutico Delta ❷ Río Paraná de las Palmas ✱✱✱: El Tropezón, Puerto La Pista, Río Hotel Laura ❸ Río Sarmiento ✱✱✱: Parque Lyfe, Museo Sarmiento, Hostería Bora Bora ❹ Río Capitán ✱✱✱: Gato Blanco, Alpenhaus, Paso del Toro, Atelier ❺ Río San Antonio ✱✱: I'Marangatu, Bar Flotante.

REFERENCES

ℹ INFORMATION ▸ PAGE 122 – BASIC DATA
🚆 TRAIN STATION ▸ PAGE 124 – TRANSPORTATION
🚌 BUS STATION ▸ PAGE 125 – TRANSPORTATION

▰ TIME TO ALLOT

🕚 **One day** will be enough time for making a stop at the proposed points.
▶ **Five hours** will be enough to travel through the five rivers.

INSCRIPTIONS
— Asphalt Road
═ Gravel Road
•••• Graded Earth Road
123 National Route
123 Provincial Route

0 Km   1   2
0 miles 0,75 1,5

SOME TIPS
Dusk is the ideal time to make a stop at one of the hostels to watch the sunset on the isles.

<table>
<tr><td>TIME TO ALLOT</td><td></td><td>Detailed Visit: three days.</td></tr>
<tr><td></td><td></td><td>Rapid Visit: two days.</td></tr>
<tr><td>DISTANCE</td><td>KM</td><td>62 km approx. (39 miles).</td></tr>
<tr><td>MEANS</td><td></td><td>Car, boat and walking.</td></tr>
</table>

Sector 3
ISLA MARTIN GARCIA

SIGHTS TO SEE

❶ Baterías 25 de Mayo ✱✱✱✱ ❷ Plaza Guillermo Brown ✱✱ ❸ Antiguo Penal ✱✱ ❹ Museo Histórico ✱ ❺ Casa de Médicos del Lazareto ✱✱ ❻ Faro ✱✱ ❼ Parque de los Héroes ✱✱✱ ❽ Barrio Chino ✱✱

Isla Martín García (Arg.)

TIME TO ALLOT

🕚 To visit Isla Martín García, the visitor may plan a entire day because a boat leaves Tigre early in the morning and returns at the end of the day.

25

Sector 1
FROM SAN ISIDRO TO TIGRE

SIGHTS TO SEE

❶ Plaza Mitre ✱✱ ❷ Catedral de San Isidro ✱✱✱✱ ❸ Colegio San Juan El Precursor ✱ ❹ Museo, Biblioteca and Archivo Municipal ✱✱ ❺ Quinta Los Ombúes ✱✱ ❻ Quinta and Museo Pueyrredón ✱✱✱ ❼ Villa Ocampo ✱✱ ❽ Monumento de los 33 Orientales ✱✱ ❾ Parque de la Costa ✱✱✱ ❿ Puerto de Frutos ✱✱✱ ⓫ Paseo Victorica ✱✱✱ ⓬ Museo Naval ✱ ⓭ Ex Tigre Club ✱✱✱ ⓮ Museo de la Reconquista ✱✱✱ ⓯ Museo de la Prefectura ✱✱

TIME TO ALLOT

🕚 This sector will take approximately five hours.

▶ Three hours will be enough to visit the most important sites.

From San Isidro to Tigre

In this itinerary along Rio de la Plata shore from San Isidro to Tigre there are lots of parks and gardens. Originally, an area of farms distributed by Juan de Garay, in 1580. In 1706, Domingo de Acassuso transformed the chapel into a public church. Twenty kilometers from the Capital City, it is one of the areas with a firmly rooted community in the Gran Buenos Aires.

⑤ QUINTA LOS OMBUES ✷✷
In 19th century, it was the property of a high society lady, Mariquita Sánchez de Thompson.

⑦ VILLA OCAMPO ✷✷
Built in 1890, by writer Victoria Ocampo's father.

① PLAZA MITRE ✷✷
It is the San Isidro central square opposite the Cathedral.

③ COLEGIO SAN JUAN EL PRECURSOR ✷
The country house belonged to Anchorena's family. Since 1957, the primary school has functioned.

⑨ PARQUE DE LA COSTA ✷✷✷

RIO DE LA PLATA

⑬ EX TIGRE CLUB ✷✷✷
Inaugurated in 1912, the first roulette functioned in Buenos Aires until 1933. Today is a cultural center.

② CATEDRAL DE SAN ISIDRO ✷✷✷✷
A parish at beginning, it became a cathedral in 1957.

⑥ QUINTA Y MUSEO PUEYRREDON ✷✷✷

WHEN THE RIVER DREAMS

ClarínX

SIGHTS TO SEE

- **CATEDRAL DE SAN ISIDRO**
- **MUSEO DE LA RECONQUISTA**
- **PUERTO DE FRUTOS**
- **PASEO VICTORICA**

FACTS

HISTORICAL TREE
José de San Martín and Martín de Pueyrredón planed their military campaigns under this carob tree in San Isidro.

⑮ MUSEO DE LA PREFECTURA ✳✳
Contains six halls devoted to the history of the naval prefecture.

⑩ PUERTO DE FRUTOS ✳✳✳
Today is a market located on the sheds of the docks.

⑭ MUSEO DE LA RECONQUISTA ✳✳✳
Created in 1948, it opened to the public in 1967.

CAZON

DEL LIBERTADOR

LUJAN

⑧ MONUMENTO A LOS 33 ORIENTALES ✳✳
In memory of the Uruguayan citizens who fought for the Independence.

⑪ PASEO VICTORICA ✳✳✳
The walk is at the shore of Luján River, located in Tigre.

⑫ MUSEO NAVAL ✳
The National Navy Museum founded in 1892 contains maps, old maritime instruments and airplanes from the Argentine Air Force.

④ MUSEO, BIBLIOTECA AND ARCHIVO MUNICIPAL ✳✳
The museum keeps the mechanism of the floral clock located on Mitre Square.

The itinerary starts in San Isidro R Station of the Tren de la Costa Line. Going along J. B. de La Salle Street is Mitre Plaza.

PLAZA MITRE | 1

Mitre Square. The most important plaza in San Isidro located at the edge of the slope surrounded by many trees, most of them tipa and lime tree planted in 1905. The traditional plaza is divided in two sectors, the lower where a floral clock was set in 1913. The clock was the first of this kind in South America constructed at the request of Mayor Adrián Beccar Varela. On the upper sector of the plaza there are many old trees and in the middle is President Bartolomé Mitre Monument erected on the occasion of the celebration of the May Revolution Centennial in 1910. On the upper level a craft fair functions during week-ends from 10 AM to 6 PM.

Ⅲ 9 DE JULIO, ITUZAINGO, JUAN B. DE LA SALLE AND LIBERTADOR AVENUE.

▶ *Crossing on the corner of Menini (9 de Julio new name on this area) and the Del Libertador Avenue is the imposing cathedral.*

Floral Clock placed on the lower level of Mitre Plaza.

CATEDRAL | 2

San Isidro Cathedral Facade.

Cathedral. Located on the grounds of the original church built in 17th Century by Domingo de Acassuso. Then San Isidro Bishopric was created in 1957 and the Cathedral consecrated as such. Declared a historical place October 10, 1963. In new Gothic style with capacity for 3,000 people, it has three naves decorated with French stained glass. The main tower is 70 meters (230 ft) in height with a clock on each side.

Ⅲ 16,200 LIBERTADOR AVENUE.

▶ *Going along 9 de Julio on the right side until finding Anchorena Street is San Juan El Precursor School.*

COLEGIO SAN | 3
JUAN EL PRECURSOR

San Juan El Precursor School. In the historical area, at one of the sides of the Cathedral was Anchorena family's country house. Erected in 1840, then remodeled in the plateresque style of the 20s by architect Estanislao Pirovano.

ELEGANT SAN ISIDRO

One of the most important train stations of De la Costa line is San Isidro R. where a shopping mall, several restaurants, two movie theaters and clothes stores are located. In the central square different shows are organized.

San Juan El Precursor School Facade.

▶ *Going back to Mitre Square, on the left side crossing Libertador Avenue is the museum.*

MUSEO, BIBLIOTECA AND ARCHIVO MUNICIPAL | 4

Municipal Museum, Library and Archive with three halls Acassuso, San Isidro Labrador and Ana Díaz exhibiting valuable objects such as a baptizing font sculpted in stone from 1778, property of the old church demolished in 1895. **III** 16,362 LIBERTADOR AV PHONE 4512-3132. HOURS: TUE THROUGH THU 8 AM TO 12 AM AND FROM 2 PM TO 6 PM. SAT AND SUN OPEN 2 PM TO 6 PM.

Patio inside the Historical Museum.

▶ *Going along Libertador Av towards Beccar Varela St, two blocks ahead after passing the Cathedral is Los Ombues country house.*

QUINTA LOS OMBUES | 5

Ombues Country House. Located opposite the De los Tres Ombúes walk, the house belonged to Mariquita Sánchez de Thompson y Mendeville. Her husband Martín Thompson gathered in the house with intellectuals of the porteño elite. The construction is from 1880 and Beccar Varela family owns the property since 1881. Dr. Cosme Varela lived and died in the house. Near the house ran the Del Norte railway, today De la Costa Line. **III** BECCAR VARELA AND BELGRANO STREET.

Ombues Country House Entrance.

▶ *Along Belgrano St to Libertador Av three blocks to the left side until reaching R. S. Peña St the Museum is on the left.*

QUINTA AND MUSEO PUEYRREDON | 6

Pueyrredón Country House and Museum. Also named the Bosque Alegre Farm, the house belonged to Brigadier Juan M. de Pueyrredón. San Martín, Sarmiento, Prilidiano Pueyrredón among other personalities were in the residence. Under the white carob tree Pueyrredón and San Martín devised the plans to liberate South America. In the galleries and in the interior there are objects belonging to the brigadier and part of the furniture that his son Prilidiano brought from Europe at the middle of 19th Century. **III** 48 RIVERA INDARTE ST. PH. 4512-3131. HOURS: TUE AND THU FROM 8 AM TO 6 PM. SAT AND SUN FROM 2 PM TO 6 PM.

Gallery in Pueyrredón Country House.

▶ *Going along Libertador Avenue to Uriburu Street, half a block on Elortondo Street is the villa.*

VILLA OCAMPO | 7

The large house built by Manuel Ocampo the writer's father; Victoria Ocam-po lived here from her childhood to her death in 1979. *Sur* Magazine Director donated the house to UNESCO in 1973. During her life, intellectuals from the world such as Ortega y Gasset among others visited the house.

29

Villa Ocampo Facade in San Isidro.

▶ *Along Lasalle to Uriburu Street on the right side at the end of the street is the monument.*

MONUMENTO A LOS 33 ORIENTALES | 8

33 Orientales Monument.

33 Orientales Monument. In 1825, the libertarian expedition named 33 Orientales headed to Uruguay; under the command of Juan Antonio Lavalleja they parted with the purpose of liberating the country from Brazilian rule. ○

Catedral de San Isidro

San Isidro Cathedral. Erected on the same grounds where Captain Domingo de Acassuso built the original chapel in 17th Century. Located in the historical center of San Isidro, the cathedral was constructed between 1895 and 1898 in new Gothic style with a remarkable tower and named after San Isidro Labrador.

THE INSIDE is 60 m (196 ft) in length with three naves forming a vast space of 1,300 sq m (1,555 sq yd) with the capacity for 3,000 people.

THE NEW GOTHIC STYLE *cathedral, containing elements of the 12th Century ogival style, was built by French architects Dunant and Paquin between 1895 and 1898. The layout is in the form of a Latincross.*

AN IMAGE OF JESUS CHRIST *on the cross is hanging from the vault.*

DUE TO THE FACT THAT *San Isidro was founded on these grounds, the Cathedral and the surrounding area is considered historical site.*

UNDERGROUND ARCHIVE
In 1895, the symbolic first stone was set along with a lead box with newspapers, coins and other objects.

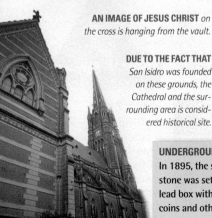

USEFUL INFORMATION

ADDRESS: 16,199 Libertador General San Martín Avenue. Telephone 4743-0291.

HOURS: The Cathedral is open Monday through Friday from 7:30 AM to 8 PM, Saturday from 8:30 AM to 8 PM. Sunday from 9AM to 10 PM.

CULTURAL ACTIVITIES: Concerts and choral performances are organized.

FACTS

THE KING'S PRESENT
In 1928, Spanish King Alfonso XIII donated a bone that belonged to the incorruptible body of San Isidro. The relic is in the Cathedral.

31

NEW GOTHIC architectural style was born mainly in France, Great Britain and Germany at the middle of 19th Century with the idea of revive the style and forms of medieval Gothic buildings. In 19th and 20th Century, Luján Basilica and La Plata Cathedral were projects inspired by this style.

NOTRE DAME OF PARIS is an example of French Gothic style.

LA PLATA CATHEDRAL is a perfect example of new Gothic style.

THE TOWER, 70 m (230 ft) in height is a point of reference for people navigating in the Rio de la Plata. It has a clock and belfry.

DOMINGO DE ACASSUSO, a pioneer in the area erected the first chapel after San Isidro Labrador had appeared during his dream.

THE CHURCH was consecrated on October 1906, two centuries after the chaplaincy had been founded.

THE PRESENT CHURCH replaced the one built by Domingo the Acassuso in 1708; the former lasted until 1895.

STAINED GLASS WINDOWS made in France decorate the interior.

SINCE 1708, the Saint Patron festivities have been celebrated with a procession every May 15.

○ *By car, the visitor will go along Uriburu to Libertador Avenue and continue along it towards Tigre. On the corner of Cazón (new name for Libertador Avenue) and Montes de Oca, then turn right, six blocks ahead is De la Costa Amusement Park.*

PARQUE DE LA COSTA | 9

Amusement Park at the shore of the river.

De la Costa Amusement Park. The station Delta of De la Costa Line is a complex containing the former station remodeled and an Amusement Park of 15 hectares (37.5 acres). Inaugurated in 1997, this park has many attractions such as a dancing water fountain, laser shows, theme restaurants and catamaran rides.

III DELTA STATION. TELEPHONE: 4732-6000. HOURS: WED - SUN AND HOLIDAYS FROM 11 AM TO 12 AM. OFF SEASON: SAT, SUN AND HOLIDAYS FROM 11 AM TO 11 PM.

CASINO TRILENIUM 👁
Located near the De la Costa Amusement Park, the casino has more than 1,500 slot machines.
It is open every day.
No admission charge.

▶ *Along Vivanco Street, two blocks on the left side towards the Capital city direction is the Tigre Fruit Port.*

PUERTO DE FRUTOS | 10

Basket Store (made of stalk or osier).

Fruit Port. Located in the large sheds of the today remodeled old port at the shore of Luján River. Originally, this market sold fruit and vegetable from the delta's orchards. Later, crafts stalls were added and the port was replaced. Today, people come to buy furniture made of reed and baskets made of osier. Craftsmen may be seen working inside of the sheds.
III 150 SARMIENTO STREET. HOURS: EVERY DAY FROM 9 AM TO 6 PM. CRAFTS FAIR: SATURDAY AND SUNDAY FROM 10 AM TO 6 PM.

▶ *Going along Sarmiento four blocks ahead until reaching Cazon Avenue the visitor will turn right four blocks to Lavalle Street, the Victorica Walk is on the right side.*

PASEO VICTORICA | 11

Sight of the Tigre Walk.

Victorica Walk. This walk on the shore of Luján River is decorated with street lamps, numerous trees, boulevards and areas for recreation. Picturesque bars and restaurants are part of the nice view of Luján River. The walk starts in Lavalle Street and ends at the mouth of Reconquista River.

▶ *Along Victorica Walk, the visitor will continue up to the number 602 where the Naval Museum and Center are located.*

MUSEO AND CENTRO NAVAL | 12

Sailboat belonging to Vito Dumas.

 Naval Museum and Center. Founded on May 20, 1892 the museum exhibits the naval and maritime history, tradition and culture of the country. The halls contain weapons, instruments for navigation and scale models of the Navy ships. Originally, the building was constructed to house the Navy's first workshops.
III 602 PASEO VICTORICA. TELEPHONE 4749-0608. HOURS: MONDAY THROUGH FRIDAY FROM 8:30 AM TO 5:30 PM. SATURDAY, SUNDAY AND HOLIDAYS FROM 10:30 AM TO 6:30 PM. GUIDED TOURS: ON WEEKENDS.

▶ *Going along the walk to the end of Victorica walk is the mouth of Reconquista River and the former Tigre Club is located.*

Patio inside the De la Reconquista Museum in Tigre.

▶ *Leaving the De la Reconquista Museum and going along Liniers Street five blocks until reaching E. Picasso Street is the Naval Prefecture Museum.*

MUSEO DE LA PREFECTURA 15

Naval Prefecture Museum.

EX TIGRE CLUB 13

Former Tigre Club. Built in 1900 by French architects Pablo Pater and Luis Dubois, in an eclectic a luxurious style. Surrounded by pergolas and balconies, today the town council and a municipal cultural center function. The admission is free. III 972 PASEO VICTORICA.

Facade of the Former Tigre Club.

▶ *Leaving the Former Tigre Club, the visitor will continue along Liniers St to Castañeda Street to find De la Reconquista Museum.*

MUSEO DE LA RECONQUISTA 14

De la Reconquista Museum. The museum is located in the place where Santiago de Liniers disembarked to conquer again the city after the first Great British invasion on August 4, 1806. The proprietor was then Martín Goyenechea. Today, it has five halls devoted to the reconquest and defense of Buenos Aires, to the history of Tigre neighborhood, to uniforms of the nation and to the former Tigre Club. In 1994, a library and an auditorium were inaugurated in the adjacent building.

III 818 LINIERS AV PH. 4512-4496. HOURS WED THROUGH SUN FROM 10 AM TO 6 PM.

Naval Prefecture Museum. The Historical Museum of the Argentine Prefecture, inaugurated on November 25, 1985 is divided into six halls devoted to history. Among the main halls there are those devoted to the first captains of Buenos Aires port and a hall of iconography where the evolution of the old premises and the present one is displayed. ■

III 1264 LINIERS AVENUE. TELEPHONE: 4749-6161. HOURS: WEDNESDAY THROUGH SUNDAY FROM 10 AM TO 12 AM AND 2 PM TO 6 PM.

33

ESTACION FLUVIAL TIGRE

Tigre Fluvial Station. *Built in English style at the shore of Luján River. The visitor will find the information about the different means of transportation going through the Delta rivers. It is here where boats sailing through the Delta depart.*

Delta de Tigre

Tigre Delta. Tigre Fluvial Station is the point of departure to travel through the five rivers in the area: Luján, Paraná de las Palmas, Capitán, Sarmiento and San Antonio. In the isles, there are many hostels, restaurants and recreational areas to spend a rewarding day of rest.

WHEN THE RIVER DREAMS

34

ClarinX

❶ RIO LUJAN ✳✳✳

Places of interest:

⬤ Centro Náutico Delta

ABRA VIEJA

CANAL VINCULACION

URION

CANAL HONDA

0km	10
0miles	6

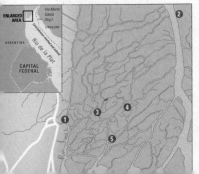

❷ RIO PARANA DE LAS PALMAS ✳✳

Places of interest:

⬤ El Tropezón

⬤ Puerto La Pista

⬤ Río Hotel Laura

⬤ El Tropezón *(on río Paraná de las Palmas)* is an example of the constructions in the Delta area.

✳ SIGHTS TO SEE

- **PARQUE LYFE**
- **ALPENHAUS**
- **MUSEO SARMIENTO**
- **I´ MARANGATU**

SEVEN DECADES OF INSCRIPTIONS
Since 1936 a record has been kept with the visitors' signatures comments and dedications, in Sarmiento Museum creating an interesting testimony.

❸ RIO SARMIENTO ✳✳✳
Places of interest:

- Parque Lyfe
- Museo Sarmiento
- Hostería Bora Bora

🔘 Museo Sarmiento *(on río Sarmiento)*. A large house protected with glass was Sarmiento's summer residence in 19th Century.

35

❹ RIO CAPITAN ✳
Places of interest:

- Gato Blanco
- Alpenhaus
- Paso del Toro
- Atelier

❺ RIO SAN ANTONIO ✳✳
Places of interest:

- I´Marangatu
- Bar flotante
- Cabañas in Puerto La Pista
  (on río Paraná de las Palmas).

🔘 Atelier is a recreational area of 5 hectares (12 acres) *(on río Capitán)* with comfortable facilities.

🔘 Alpenhaus *(on río Capitán)* is a hostel in German style with bungalows.

The sector starts in Tigre Fluvial Station. From where the boats sailing through the Delta isles depart.

RIO LUJAN `1`

Before flowing into the Río de la Plata river, the Luján river extends along urban areas such as Tigre and San Fernando. The best recreational area is the Nautical Center, half an hour by boat from the Fluvial Station.

⫶ EMPRESA FLUVIAL DELTA ARGENTINO. TELEPHONE 4749-0537.

Grocery Store in El Tropezón Hostel.

CENTRO NAUTICO DELTA ①

Delta Nautical Center. It is the ideal place to spend a day in a place with paddle courts, three swimming pools, sandy beaches, barbecue, etc. Visitors can rent boats and trycicles.

⫶ TELEPHONE 4728-0410.

RIO PARANA `2`

Paraná River. The Paraná de las Palmas was named after the numerous palms planted along its shore. To arrive at this arm of the river, the visitor will sail approximately one-half hour.

⫶ EMPRESA DELTA ARGENTINO.

HAROLDO CONTI

Writer Haroldo Conti lived years in the Delta, he described its inhabitants in his novel *Sudeste*: "They resemble the river. They do not exactly love it, they only could not live without the river".

EL TROPEZON ①

Built in 1928, it was a fashionable spot in 1930 and many tourists visited the premises. The dinning room has a large window facing a typical park from the Delta. Due to its dimensions and preserved facilities the building is an example of the isles architecture.

⫶ TELEPHONE 4728-1012.

THE WILD SIDE OF THE DELTA

An alternative to the traditional tours is adventure and ecological tourism with boat rides along rivers and streams, trekking on woods, camping, picture safaris and visits to historical sites.

⫶ INFORMATION: TELEPHONE 4512-4497.

PUERTO LA PISTA ②

La Pista is a small hotel with four comfortable cabanas facing the river, equipped with kitchen, bathroom, running water. The place has six sandy beaches. Visitors may rent canoes, kayaks or boats to sail through the river.

⫶ TELEPHONE: 4728-2108.

RIO HOTEL LAURA ③

Rio Hotel Laura Restaurant.

Rio Hotel Laura was inaugurated in 1907 and is the oldest and most traditional in the isles of the Tigre Delta area. The hotel has verdant areas, comfortable rooms and bungalows, a swimming pool and a bar. The restaurant located in an English style house has a terrace facing the river.

⫶ TELEPHONE: 4749 3898.

LEOPOLDO LUGONES

Februrary 18, 1938, writer Leopoldo Lugones committed suicide in one of the rooms of El Tropezón. From then, the owners dedicated the room to his memory and a carved stone by the river. The writer's note on the eve of the event is also kept on the premises.

RIO SARMIENTO | 3

Sarmiento River. One of the most navigated of the Delta area. On its shore there are many houses and clubs, thus many public and private boat sail on the waters, specially on weekends. III EMPRESA INTERISLEÑA. ADDRESS: 499 LAVALLE STREET. TELEPHONE: 4731-0261/0262/0263. SATURDAY, SUNDAY AND HOLIDAY: 419 LAVALLE STREET. TELEPHONE 4731-0264.

PARQUE LYFE (1)

Located on 4 hectares with camping area, showers, a market, broilers, volley courts and a sandy beach. There is a section for children with a playground. III TELEPHONE: 4728-0073.

MUSEO SARMIENTO (2)

Desk in Sarmiento Museum.

Sarmiento Museum. President Domingo Faustino Sarmiento built the house in 1855 for vacationing. On September 11, 1997 the museum was created. A glass-covered structure preserves the building. In the interior, there are furniture and personal objects of the President. Municipal Public Library Paula Albarracín functions here. Near the house is a prefabricated house in English style of the beginning of 20th Century where the Association for the Protection of Children, Birds and Plants functioned; Sarmiento bought the house in 1855.

HOSTERIA BORA BORA (3)

Solarium in Bora Bora Hostel.

Bora Bora Hostel. Located 80 meters (88 yards) from the shore, it is necessary to cross a bridge to enter the premises. There is a lagoon near the river, a sandy beach and a swimming pool. The hostel rooms have heating system and private bathroom. The sitting room has play games. ◯ III TELEPHONE 4728-0646.

Sight of Parque Lyfe Facade.

o *Leaving the Tigre Fluvial Station by boat, there are two possibilities, to navigate through Capitán River or through San Antonio River.*

RIO CAPITAN | 4

Capitán River. It starts on the confluence of Sarmiento River and Abra Vieja stream. Further on, the waters of San Antonio River join the flow where Victoria isle is located to finally end in Paraná de las Palmas. The woods at the shores are covered with poplar and willow trees. Many wooded docks to go into restaurants and recreational areas can be seen along the traject.

III PUBLIC BOATS. EMPRESA INTERISLEÑA. TELEPHONE: 4749-0900.

GATO BLANCO

Gato Blanco Outdoor Dinning Room.

The traditional restaurant is located on the right side after passing Victoria isle. It has a pri-

WICKER WORK

The island inhabitants cultivate this flexible twig for manufacturing wicker work. President Sarmiento favored the growing of this flexible plant of willow or osier when he planted the first twig in the area on September 8, 1855. Today 80 or 90% of wicker works are manufactured in the Delta.

vate dock and a restaurant for 150 people serving international dishes and excellent broiled meat. Besides, the teahouse is famous for the excellent homemade cakes and pastries. There are also volley courts and a children playground.

III TELEPHONE: 4728-0390.

ALPENHAUS

Located in Rama Negra stream and Capitán River confluence. The premises have 2,500 sq m (2,990 sq yd) surface containing a huge park and a private dock. This European style construction offers lodging in bungalows with Jacuzzi and mini gym. The restaurant offers German and Austrian specialties. Alpenhaus

is the center for the celebration of the Beer Festival in the Delta each November.

III TELEPHONE 4728-0422.

PASO DEL TORO

Children Playground in Paso del Toro.

Bull's Trea. The restaurant may be easily spotted by the large white bull on the river shore and is open only on weekends. The facilities include a park and a playground for children. Homemade pastas are the house speciality and the ravioli are highly recommended.

III TELEPHONE: 4728-0775.

ATELIER

The hostel and restaurant are located on a surface of 5 hectares (12 acres). The visitor may walk around the premises, take sun on the chairs on the

Motorboat in front of Apenhaus Hostel, of German style.

sandy beaches. It has a private dock and heliport. The bungalows are very comfortable with television and microwave oven. On the restaurant menu are notable cold dishes, assorted cheese and excellent homemade pasta. ||| TELEPHONE: 4728-0043.

Atelier Facilities Entrance.

RIO SAN ANTONIO | 5

It is an important arm of Sarmiento River in the area known as Tres Bocas. San Antonio river ends in the Urión river further north. On its shore there is a residential area where houses, hostels, recreational facilities and restaurants are located.
||| PASSENGER BOATS. EMPRESA INTERISLEÑA. TELEPHONE 4749-0900.

LANCHAS COLECTIVAS
Public Boats. These boats for public transportation and excursions have almost one hundred people capacity. The visitor may watch the landscape through large windows.

I'MARANGATU ①

The restaurant and hostel is mainly visited by young people. Therefore, the owners chose a Brazilian name to recreate the ambience of the beaches in that country. The central building

The platforms in the Bar Flotante, a superb view of the coast.

resembles a Mediterranean style house. The restaurant and the bar offer excellent services and the cabanas to spend the night are comfortable. The facilities contain volley and soccer court and a swimming pool. There is also a water ski school providing gear and motorboats to practice the sport.
||| TELEPHONE 4728-0752.

BAR FLOTANTE ②

To arrive at Floating Bar is necessary to go by private boat or taxi boat. It contains two floating platforms serving fast food and snacks. Besides the excellent food, the visitor may enjoy a beautiful sight of San Isidro coast from there.
||| TELEPHONE. 4728-0752. ■

THE PAINTER IN LOVE WITH THE DELTA

Alejandro Schulz Solari (1887-1963), known as Xul Solar, died in his Delta house, a place he loved immensely.
Son of a Lithuanian and a Genoese lady, Xul Solar was born in San Fernando. When he was 14 years old he boarded a ship as a stowaway and traveled through Europe. In 1924 he returned to his country and became an artist of the avant-garde. Self educated, he spoke many languages and was interested in diverse areas from mathematics to astrology.

Islas del Delta de Tigre

Tigre Delta Isles. The first part up to Paraná de las Palmas River has 220 sq kilometers (543 acres) corresponding to Tigre jurisdiction divided in hundreds of isles. It is one of the favorite spots for visiting on weekends due to the diversity of the landscape, the presence of recreational areas and sport facilities.

SEEDS AND FRUIT collected along the river's length are deposited on the delta creating a diverse vegetal life.

WATER HYACINTH FLOWER *usually appears during spring and summer.*

THE MOST COMMON TREES *on the shore of the isles are timbo, bay tree, ceiba, criollo willow, guava tree, ñangarapi among others.*

CAPYBARA, *the largest amphibious rodent in the world.*

THE LOCAL FAUNA has amphibious mammals like capybara, the yacaré, a reptile similar to an alligator. There are plenty of aquatic birds. The marsh deer *(photo)* is in danger of extinction.

DIFFERENT BIRD SPECIES *are seen in the Delta area such as coots and white heron (right).*

USEFUL INFORMATION

ESTACION FLUVIAL DE TIGRE: 305 Mitre Avenue.
SERVICES: From Estación Fluvial de Tigre leave public boats covering different routes and catamarans for programmed excursions. The visitor will also find taxi boats.
HOURS: Public Boats return to the station between 4 PM and 6:30 PM.

FACTS

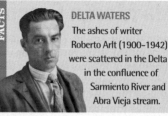

DELTA WATERS
The ashes of writer Roberto Arlt (1900–1942) were scattered in the Delta in the confluence of Sarmiento River and Abra Vieja stream.

TAXI BOATS *are more expensive than public boat, the boats are ideal for short journeys for groups of four to six people.*

HOSTELS have restaurants, rooms, sport and recreational facilities to spend a day or to stay overnight. Atelier *(photo)* has 5 hectares (more than 12 acres) of terrain.

41

THE LOCAL POPULATION *has a special infrastructure such as schools with docks (photo) and boats selling groceries around the area.*

THE RECREATIONAL ESTABLISH-MENTS on the shores are prepared to receive people in their solarium and water sports facilities.

IN THE ISLES *there are 5,000 dwellings, 40 restaurants and 3,500 inhabitants. The hotels have 300 beds.*

BOATS *are the most common means of transportation in the area.*

Isla Martín García

Martín García Island. This two square kilometers island (0.8 sq miles), discovered during Juan Díaz de Solís expedition in 1516, is located in the Río de la Plata three hours of navigation from Buenos Aires. Verdant woods surround the little town. Between 1930 and 1963 four Argentine President were imprisoned in the island.

❽ BARRIO CHINO ✳✳
In 17th and 18th Centuries sailors disembarking in the island went to this part of the island to look for prostitutes, they called them "chinas" (chinese women). The term did not designate women from the oriental country.

❼ PARQUE A LA MEMORIA DE LOS HEROES COMUNES A AMBOS PUEBLOS ✳✳
Sarmiento ordered poplar trees to be planted throughout the park.

❹ MUSEO HISTORICO ✳
Created by the inhabitants with the collaboration of the Navy, it keeps objects of daily life.

0km		2
0miles		1,5

❶ BATERIA 25 DE MAYO ✳✳✳✳
Erected by Sarmiento when the Triple Alianza war started (1865-1870).

✳ SIGHTS TO SEE

- **BATERIAS 25 DE MAYO**
- **RESERVA NATURAL**
- **ANTIGUO PENAL**
- **BARRIO CHINO**

FACTS

DARIO'S MUSE
Nicaraguan poet Ruben Dario lodged in the octagonal house of the Quarantine Hospital during his visit to the island and wrote *La Marcha Triunfal*.

43

❻ THE LIGHTHOUSE ✴
In 1881, during Julio Argentino Roca presidency, the lighthouse was erected. Two years later the Maritime Vigilance Service was created.

❺ CASA DE MEDICOS DEL LAZARETO ✴✴
Immigrants arriving to the island were imposed a quarantine.

❽ ANTIGUO PENAL ✴✴
Built in 19th Century, there was a section for military prisoners. It functioned until 1960.

❷ PLAZA ALMIRANTE BROWN ✴✴
In this central part of the town, the navy combatant is remembered.

Leaving the Tigre Fluvial Station, the visitor will navigate three hours to arrive at Martín García Island; descending on the dock is 25 de Mayo Battery.

BATERIAS 25 DE MAYO `1`

25 de Mayo Battery. Domingo Faustino Sarmiento ordered the installation of these four defensive constructions in 1868. Then the armed conflict called Triple Alianza ensued and the war against Paraguay deepened. The three English cannons Todman located on the place were fired only to salute. In 1905, they were fired for the last time to pay honors to President José Figueroa Alcorta on the occasion of his visit.

25 de Mayo Battery and the Cannons.

▶ *Leaving 25 de Mayo Battery, going along the path a couple of meters ahead Guillermo Brown Plaza is located on the left side.*

MARTIN GARCIA ◉
The island is named after a steward who was part of Juan de Solís expedition in 1516. García died on board and later was buried in the island.

Ruins of the Old Penitentiary. There only remain the exterior walls.

PLAZA GUILLERMO BROWN `2`

Guillermo Brown Plaza.

Guillermo Brown Square. The most important plaza in the island, at one of the sides is the civic center where the post offices and other administrative office function. In this building President Hipólito Yrigoyen was a prisoner after being deposed in 1930.

▶ *At the end of the plaza, the visitor will first turn right and then left to arrive at the Penitentiary.*

ANTIGUO PENAL `3`

Old Penitentiary. On April 24, 1765 the first naval and military prison was erected. The facilities were constructed to imprison seven deserters from Buenos Aires Battalion. Later, the number of prisoners increased and they were forced to erect constructions in the island. The prisoners also extracted stones from a quarry to be used in the streets of Buenos Aires. The facilities functioned as penitentiary until 1957 when they were dismantled. Today there only remain some stone walls from the old prison. ◉

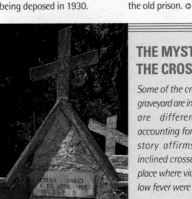

THE MYSTERY OF THE CROSSES

Some of the crosses in the graveyard are inclined. There are different stories accounting for this fact. A story affirms that the inclined crosses mark the place where victims of yellow fever were buried.

The Island of the Prisoners

Isla Martín García was used on several occasions to confine political prisoners. Four Argentine Presidents were incarcerated on the island. People believed they were in the Penitentiary but the truth is they were in the island's dwellings under vigilance.

◀ **HIPOLITO YRIGOYEN** was 78 years old when he was confined in the island accompanied by his daughter Elena in 1930. He was liberated in 1933, a little after he died.

1930

On September 6, General F. Uriburu overthrew Yrigoyen a sent him to the island.

▲ **THE RECORD BOOK** lists Yrigoyen's problems of health during his banishment.

1932

The Radicalismo and other political parties disclosed the fraudulent elections of the conservative government.

▶ **MARCELO T. DE ALVEAR** was imprisoned four months in the island accused of conspiring against Agustín P. Justo conservative government in 1932.

◀ **JUAN DOMINGO PERON** was compelled to resign to his post in Edelmiro J. Farrel government and sent to the isle on October 13, 1945.

◀ **ARTURO FRONDIZI**
In 1962 he was sent to the island after being overthrown, a year later was sent to Bariloche.

1945

October 17, the Argentine people went to the street to demand the liberation of General Perón. From then, the day to the Peronist loyalty is celebrated.

1962

There was an internal fight between the militaries who organize a coup d'etat against President Frondizi. The blue faction defeated the red ones.

○ Opposite the ruins of the old penitentiary on the corner located diagonally is Almirante Brown Plaza and the Island Historical Museum.

MUSEO HISTORICO | 4

Historical Museum. The Museum was created by initiative of the local inhabitants, accordingly the islanders daily implements are exhibited. Among the objects exhibited in the museum, the visitor will find furniture donated by the islanders, old photographs. There are also historical documents of the Argentine Navy and cannon bullets exhibited on the premises. It is worthwhile mentioning a sanitary toilet Marcelo Torcuato de Alvear ordered to be brought from Buenos Aires during his confinement in 1932; the implement constitutes an oddity. On the same grounds was located the island old pulpería.

Exhibition Hall in the Historical Museum in Martín García Island.

▓ THE MUSEUM IS OPEN WHEN THE BOAT WITH PASSENGERS ARRIVE TO THE ISLAND.

▶ Going along the same street the visitor will turn left, on the same block is the physicians' house in the Quarantine Hospital.

CASA DE MEDICOS | 5
DEL LAZARETO

Quarantine Hospital. The house of the physicians practicing medicine in the Quarantine Hospital belongs to the end of 19th Century. Since then until 1915 a hospital for treating victims of different epidemics suffered in Buenos Aires functioned. Besides, passengers arriving from ships were imposed a quarantine before going to the city. Luis Agote was one of the directors, he discovered that blood could be put aside for transfusing in 1914. Poet Rubén Darío stayed in the house during his visit to the island; a manuscript of his is exhibited in the museum. Today, the island ecological center functions displaying illustrations on the subject.

Physician's house in the Quarantine Hospital.

▶ Going along the street and turning left, the visitor will continue a block and turn right on the following until arriving at the next corner, a block ahead is the lighthouse on the right side.

THE NATIONAL PARK

Since 1974 Martín García is a national park; in 1988 it was declared a reserve for multiple purposes. The environment, a peripheral forest contains animal species such as the American alligator (overo) and has changed after the arrival of human beings.

LIGHTHOUSE 6

Old Lighthouse in the Island.

A very old lighthouse, Martín García beam was installed in 1881 during Julio Argentino Roca presidency. Its lights oriented seaman approaching the island and guided them through canals, reefs or barriers on the mouth of Uruguay River. Since 1927 it is out of service.

▶ *On the corner of the lighthouse, the visitor will turn left and go along the street three blocks until arriving at one of the edges of the Memorial Park to the Heroes.*

PARQUE A 7
LOS HEROES

Memorial Park to the Heroes of Both Countries. The Memorial to the heroes of both countries offers the visitor the possibility to wander through paths filled with old trees, bamboo field, sandy grounds and cane field. Located near the coast, the monument pays homage to the Rio de la Plata Treaty undersigned by both countries, Uruguay and Argentina in 1974. During the ceremony of inauguration of the monument the flags of the countries undersigning the treat-

LA PANADERIA

The Bakery. *In an old house from 1913 the only bakery at the island functions. The place is famous due to its singular architectural style and one of the specialties, a Christmas cake famous beyond the island limits. The owner wanted to sell a product identifying the island.*

ment were hoisted. The long path leading to the monument is planted with many poplars put in the ground during Domingo F. Sarmiento presidency.

AMERICA'S CAPITAL
In 1851, Domingo Faustino Sarmiento disembarked in Martín García Island, he wrote on a rock the name Argirópolis or Ciudad del Plata; his dream was to have a Capital city for the United States of South America.

▶ *In one of the edges of the Memorial Park, on a street leading to the river coast is Chinatown.*

BARRIO CHINO 8

Empty houses in Chinatown.

Chinatown. A group of abandoned houses covered by vegetation. Originally, it was a modest neighborhood often visited by sailors looking for prostitutes called by them chinas. A term used since the times of the Colony to designate mestizo women, it was also used with affectionate meaning. ■

47

Different natural environments in the Memorial Park to the Heroes.

The Plains

The immensity of the Pampean Plains appears when Buenos Aires is lost in the country. From flowery Escobar at the shore of the Parana river the horizon is opened to the emblematic and religious Luján and to San Antonio de Areco and its estancias.

DEL PILAR CHURCH

SAN ANDRÉS DE GILES MUSEUM

ESTANCIA EL OMBU

ESTANCIA LA CINACINA

HALL IN MUSEO RICARDO GÜIRAL

HERMITAGE IN ESTANCIA LA PORTEÑA

ESTANCIA LA BAMBA

MUSEO RICARDO GUIRALDES

SAN ANTONIO DE ARECO AGRICULTURAL LAND

BASILICA DE LUJAN

From Escobar to San Antonio de Areco

This itinerary traveling through the pampas in Buenos Aires province is divided in two sectors. The first one goes from Escobar to San Andrés de Giles. The monumental Basílica de Luján and the Museo del Transporte are noteworthy. The second includes San Antonio de Areco and its surroundings where a day in the country may be relished in different estancias; the Museum Gauchesco Ricardo Güiraldes devot-ed to gauchos and the legendary estancia La Porteña are remarkable.

Sector 1
ESCOBAR TO SAN ANDRES DE GILES

SIGHTS TO SEE

❶ Escobar ✱✱✱: Plaza a los Héroes de Malvinas, Plaza Juan Manuel de Rosas, Jardín Japonés ❷ Lugar del Milagro ✱✱ ❸ Pilar ✱✱✱: Cruz del Pilar, Plaza 12 de Octubre, Iglesia Nuestra Señora del Pilar ❹ Luján ✱✱✱✱: Basílica de Luján, Museo del Transporte, Museo Histórico Nacional ❺ San Andrés de Giles ✱✱

SOME TIPS
It is advisable to travel this itinerary during a weekend, wearing comfortable clothes and bring some clothes to ride a horse in the estancias.

Sector 2
SAN ANTONIO DE ARECO

SIGHTS TO SEE

❶ San Antonio de Areco ✱✱✱: Museo Gasparini, Centro Cultural and Museo Usina Vieja, Museo Gauchesco Ricardo Güiraldes, puente viejo ❷ Estancia La Cinacina ✱✱✱ ❸ Estancia La Porteña ✱✱✱ ❹ Estancia El Ombú de Areco ✱✱✱ ❺ Estancia La Bamba ✱✱

INSCRIPTIONS
—— Asphalt Road
═══ Gravel Road
•••••• Graded Earth Road
[123] National Route
[123] Provincial Route

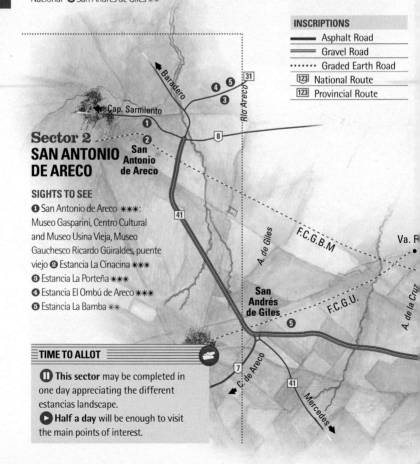

TIME TO ALLOT

⓫ **This sector** may be completed in one day appreciating the different estancias landscape.
▶ **Half a day** will be enough to visit the main points of interest.

TIME TO ALLOT	⏸	Detailed Visit: two days.
	▶	Rapid Visit: one day.
DISTANCE	KM	116 km approx. (72 miles).
MEANS	🚗	By car and walking.

Enlarged Area

S. Antonio de Areco — B. de Escobar — Pilar — **9**

8

S. Andrés de Giles — Luján

7

CAPITAL FEDERAL

N

0 Km — 20 — 40
0 miles — 12.5 — 25

TIME TO ALLOT

⏸ **In one day** the sector may be visited at a relaxed pace.

▶ **Half a day** will be enough to cover the entire sector without going into churches and museums.

Río Luján

Belén de Escobar ➊

A. Burgueño

Capital Federal

9

Río Luján

Matheu

25

Va. Rosa ➋

Capital Federal

Pilar Indutrial Park

Zelaya

8

6

Fátima

Pilar

8

➌

Torres

6

Open Door

A. de las Palomas

28

Capital Federal

Carlos Keen

Luján

➎

7

➍

6

0 Km — 5 — 10
0 miles — 3 — 6

F.C.G.S.M.

Mercedes

REFERENCES

ℹ️ INFORMATION •▶ PAGE 122 – BASIC DATA
🚉 TRAIN STATION •▶ PAGE 124 – TRANSPORTATION
🚌 BUS STATION •▶ PAGE 125 – TRANSPORTATION
⛽ GAS STATION

51

Escobar to San Andrés de Giles

This sector goes from the shores of the Paraná River to the Pampean area of the Buenos Aires province. It starts in Escobar, the National Capital of the Flower, and continues in Luján: catholic landmark and peregrination center with the imposing Basilica. The itinerary ends in superb and extensive rural landscapes.

LA POSTA DE FIGUEROA

Figueroa Post. In 1755 a post for horses in San Andrés de Giles was founded; in the 18th Century the post service changed horses in this site.

❺ SAN ANDRES DE GILES ✶✶

This town is well-known by its museum complex and San Andrés church.

0km		5
0miles		3

❺

❼

RIO LUJAN

❹

❹ LUJAN ✶✶✶✶

Places of interest:
- ⬤ Basílica de Luján
- ⬤ Museo del Transporte
- ⬤ Museo Colonial e Histórico

⬤ San Martín's *poncho* exhibited in the Museo Colonial e Histórico *(Luján).*

⬤ Basílica de Luján *(Luján),* in new Gothic style was erected in 1930.

⬤ Museo del Transporte *(Luján)* exhibits old carriages.

✴ SIGHTS TO SEE

- **IGLESIA NUESTRA SEÑORA DEL PILAR**
- **BASILICA DE LUJAN**
- **MUSEO DEL TRANSPORTE**
- **MUSEO COLONIAL E HISTORICO**

FACTS

A MUSEUM ON HORSEBACK
Saddles and trappings made of leather or woven fabrics used by gauchos are exhibited in Yancamil Museum.

❶ ESCOBAR ✳✳✳

Places of interest:
- Plaza a los Héroes de Malvinas
- Plaza Juan Manuel de Rosas
- Jardín Japonés

❷ SITE OF THE MIRACLE ✳✳

This house was the first Virgen de Luján sanctuary and contains a replica of the image.

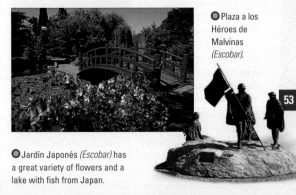

● Plaza a los Héroes de Malvinas *(Escobar)*.

● Jardín Japonés *(Escobar)* has a great variety of flowers and a lake with fish from Japan.

53

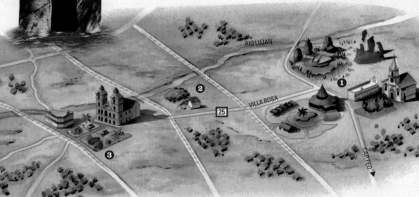

RIO LUJAN

VILLA ROSA

25

CAP FED

● Plaza 12 de Octubre *(Pilar)* was declared historical site in 1942.

● Cruz del Pilar *(Pilar)* remembers the crucifix made of a trunk of the tree by Jesuitical missionaries in 1790.

❸ PILAR ✳✳✳

Places of interest:
- Cruz del Pilar
- Plaza 12 de Octubre
- Iglesia Nuestra Señora del Pilar

● The colonial baroque Nuestra Señora del Pilar *(Pilar)* has a Way of the Cross from 1600.

THE PLAINS

54

ClarínX

This sector starts in Escobar, a nice old town located on the northwest part of Buenos Aires on kilometer number fifty of the Panamericana Route.

ESCOBAR | 1

After Buenos Aires foundation in 1580, Juan de Garay distributed the lands alocating plots to his men. Don Alonso de Escobar was a Creole *(criollo)*, born in Asunción del Paraguay and Garay awarded him with a plot. Therefore, the town and the railway station are named after him. These lands, inhabited mainly by Spanish and *Criollos* at that time were under the jurisdiction of the Villa de Luján Cabildo until October 8, 1859 when the town became municipality and Belén de Escobar was the main district.

PLAZA A LOS HEROES DE MALVINAS

Malvinas Heroes Monument.

Malvinas Heroes Square. The plaza was inaugurated April 18, 1997 in memory of the four soldiers from Escobar fallen in Malvinas (Falklands Islands) war in 1982. Ernesto Audivert designed the monument and Ernesto Bertedro started the construction. Former combatants in the Falklands Islands war watch over this emblematic plaza.

III INDEPENDENCIA AND 25 DE MAYO.

PLAZA JUAN MANUEL DE ROSAS ②

Brigadier Juan Manuel de Rosas Plaza.

The Brigadier Juan Manuel de Rosas Square was inaugurated October 24, 1997. Sculptor Julio César Domínguez designed the plaza inspired in 19th Century gardens. When strolling around rose bushes and jasmine flowers, the colonial times come back to memory. From the kiosk, beautiful flowers can be appreciated. The gardener is dressed with a replica of the red garment worn by Rosas' militia. Rosas' sculpture in the plaza is the only complete figurine of the President in the whole country.

III ALBERDI STREET BETWEEN TAPIA DE CRUZ STREET AND SPADACCINI STREET.

JARDIN JAPONES ③

Japanese Garden. The garden was inaugurated on October 4, 1996. The large Japanese community of Escobar made and donated the garden on the occasion of the four hundred anniversary of the settlement of this ethnic group in the city. Most of the lanterns and the fish in the pond were brought from Japan with funds granted by Japanese citizens to create this classic style park. The Japanese garden is placed on the grounds of the Town Hall where different institutions function such as the civil courts, the civil registry, a center for sport activities and a cultural center.

III ALBERDI ST. AND SPADACCINI ST. HOURS IN WINTER: SUNDAY THROUGH THURSDAY FROM 9 AM TO 7 PM. FRIDAY, SATURDAY AND HOLIDAY FROM 10 AM TO 8 PM.

FLOWER CAPITAL ◉

In 1964, President Arturo Illia passed a decree declaring Escobar National Capital of the Flower. Every year, a celebration in the flower exhibition hall is held.

View from inside of the Japanese Garden in Escobar.

ZOO MUNCHI´S

Munchi's Zoo in Escobar is a natural space with walks and an artificial lake where the visitor may appreciate more than one thousand bird species. Besides, many farm animals are exhibited in the zoo. ▌▌▌ ROUTE 25 AND MIGUEL CANE STREET. INFORMATION: TELEPHONE (03488) 42-4901.

55

▶ *Leaving Escobar, the visitor will follow Route 25 towards Pilar. In Villa Rosa, turn left to Zelaya where the Place of the Miracle is found.*

LUGAR DEL MILAGRO

The Place of the Miracle. In 1630, a wagon transporting a Virgin image to Santiago del Estero was trapped in the mud. When the imaged was unloaded from the wagon the bullocks resumed the journey. People interpreted the fact as an omen and thought the Virgin would remain there. The believers built this adobe house in Villa Rosa town and designated a slave to watch over the Virgin. In 1671, the original image was transported to Luján area. ▌▌▌ ROUTE 25, VILLA ROSA. TELEPHONE 4791-2622. MASS: MONDAY THROUGH FRIDAY AT 9 AM IN WINTER AND AT 8 AM IN SUMMER. SATURDAY AND SUNDAY FROM 11 AM TO 12 PM.

▶ *Leaving the Miracle site, the visitor will return to Route 25 and turn right to continue 10 kilometers ahead to Pilar.*

Modest dwelling of the person who watched over the Virgin.

PILAR

The history of the place started in 1580 and is reflected in its centennial buildings that still can be appreciated. On October 24 of that year, Juan de Garay distributed land and estancias and gave Antonio Bermúdez number eight that included a large part of Pilar jurisdiction. The first inhabitants came in 1673 when the construction of Santa María de la Concepción del Río Luján Fort in Corpus Christi valley started, however the construction was never completed. In 1818, the Buenos Aires Cabildo authorized the relocation of old Pilar to the present grounds at the shore of Lujan River. The new founder was Lorenzo López; the district was created with the same name in 1821.

TRATADO DEL PILAR
Pilar Treaty. Signed February 23, 1820, it is the origin of federalism. Due to this event, Pilar is known as the cradle of federalism.

CRUZ DEL PILAR ①

Pilar Cross. In 1790, Jesuitical missionaries spreading the word of Jesus along the territory were on their way to the north of the country and stopped on this area. They erected a cross made of a trunk in order to pray for the recovery of their brothers and for a safe journey. Afterwards, the cross was built in concrete and surrounded by an iron fence.

The Cross of the Pilar Jesuits.

PLAZA 12 DE OCTUBRE

The plaza is located opposite the Municipal Palace in the center of the city. In 1942, this open area was declared an historical site due to the fact that on these grounds the Pilar Treaty was signed. Many statues and other monuments decorate the verdant space such as *The mother* a bust by sculptor Luis Perlotti supported by a superb pillar, the Pilar Virgin statue and a cross devoted to Evangelization in America blessed by Pope John Paul II.

Main Nave in Pilar Church.

Flags in 12 de Octubre Plaza.

IGLESIA NUESTRA SEÑORA DEL PILAR

Nuestra Señora del Pilar Church. The church was erected in the 19th Century. In 1821, architect José Villa started the construction using mud; subsequently in 1840 the main nave and the upper floors were made of lime. The style of the temple is baroque and inside there is a way of the cross made in Italy in 1600. In the interior is the Pilar Virgin image brought from Saragossa, Spain.

▮▮▮ LORENZO LOPEZ AND BELGRANO STREET.

▶ *Along Route 8 until crossing Route 6, the visitor will turn left 21 km until reaching Route 7, then 8 km ahead is Luján.*

LUJAN | 4

Luján was founded a little time after the colonization of Buenos Aires countryside had started. It is named after Captain Pedro de Luján, member of an expedition sent by Pedro de Mendoza after founding Buenos Aires in 1536. Amerindians murdered the Captain at the shores of the river that today has his name. Luján was the most important city of many towns and boroughs set up during colonial times. At the end of 17th Century and without official planning, the town developed around the Virgen de Luján Sanctuary before the rest of the places in the area. The sanctuary was previous to the erection of the Basilica.

BASILICA DE LUJAN

Luján Basilica Facade.

Luján Basilica is considered a personal achievement of Father Jorge Salvaire, born in Tarn, France. The priest participated actively in the project. On May 15, 1887 the first symbolic stone for the construction was blessed; in 1890 the foundations were laid and the construction was completed by French architect Ulderico Courtois in 1930. This new Gothic style and ogival building was consecrated archdiocese by Pope John Paul II. It is in the fourth place toge-ther with the cathedrals of Barcelona, Marseille in France and Winnipeg in Canada, all of similar characteristics.

RURAL RAILROAD

On May 24, 1889 San Andrés de Giles town was proud to open its first railway. People called it the rural Tramway. The first travel covered the route Buenos Aires–San Andrés de Giles departing from Buenos Aires with a car of iron wheels pulled by horse.

•▸ MORE INFORMATION PAGE 58.

MUSEO DEL TRANSPORTE ②

Transportation Museum. The museum has the most comprehensive collection of carriages in Argentina. Among the most outstanding transports are *La Porteña*, the first steam-engine locomotive originally from Great Britain, the seaplane *Plus Ultra* from Germany that made the journey from Spain with pilot Ramón Franco in 1925 and Juan Manuel de Rosas' family sulky. In addition to all this transports, there is *Legh*, Vito Dumas' boat, the solitary seaman who navigate around the whole world.

▐ 917 LEZICA STREET AND TORREZURI STREET. TELEPHONE 42-0245. HOURS. WEDNESDAY THROUGH FRIDAY FROM 12:15 PM TO 5:30 PM. SUNDAY 10:15 AM TO 6:30 PM.

La Porteña locomotive steam engine, exhibited in Luján Transportation Museum.

MUSEO COLONIAL E HISTORICO ③

Colonial Museum Interior Patio.

Colonial and Historical Museum. Located near the Town Hall, the colonial construction from 18th Century functioned as the Villa del Luján Cabildo created by Spanish King Fernando VI. British soldiers who participated in the 1806 invasion were imprisoned in the house. In 1821, Domingo Beschetedt, an officer of the Luján Municipality made all kinds of efforts to avoid the demolishing of the building and succeeded. The Museum was

LUJAN PARK 👁

A couple of meters from the Basilica is the Lujan Park with an aerial tramway going along the river coast.

officially inaugurated on April 28, 1918. Today, the museum contains halls devoted to the Cabildo's history, the Viceroy's house and Paraguay War. It also has a hall devoted to customs and traditions of the *gaucho* containing silver works and the history of *mate* and *pulperias*.

▐ 917 LEZICA STREET AND TORREZURI STREET. TELEPHONE: 42-0245. HOURS: WEDNESDAY THROUGH FRIDAY FROM 12:15 PM TO 5:30 AM. SATURDAY AND SUNDAY FROM 10:15 AM TO 6:30 PM.

▶ *Along Route 7, 39 kilometers ahead is San Andrés de Giles.*

SAN ANDRES DE GILES |5

On November 30, 1806, the anniversary of the town, Father Vicente Iñero celebrated the first mass in a chapel erected on grounds granted by Francisco de Suero y Giles, in such a way the town was born. In 1821, the first inhabitants made possible to appoint the first authority, a mayor from the brotherhood. In 1830, the borough was created and San Andrés de Giles became a city in 1937. Among the remarkable points of interest for paying a visit are Figueroa Post, the interesting Museum complex, San Martín Plaza designed by Vicente Piñero, Bishop Escalada cross and San Andrés church located on the grounds of the first oratory. ∎

Interior Sight of San Andrés de Giles Museum Complex.

Basílica de Luján

Luján Basilica. The most important of the Roman Catholic Church in Argentina, it is an imposing new Gothic style church located in Plaza Belgrano in Luján. Every year in May and October, millions of pilgrims come from all America.

ITS 19 BELLS *were cast in iron of cannons used in First World War.*

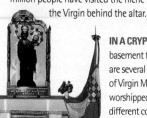

THE TOWERS *are 106 m (348 ft) in height and each one has a clock.*

THE MAIN ALTAR, donated by Armstrong family at the beginning of 20th Century is made of marble, bronze and gold. Eight million people have visited the niche with the Virgin behind the altar.

IN A CRYPT on the basement there are several images of Virgin Mary worshipped in different countries of the world.

THE TWO ORGANS *are both valuable European instruments, the largest has 5,800 pipes.*

GOTHIC STYLE, *Father Salvaire and Archbishop Aneiros had the idea of erecting a church inspired in French cathedrals and French architect Ulderico Courtois directed the project.*

THE STONES *in the constructions were extracted from a quarry, property of the church in Colón, Entre Ríos.*

USEFUL INFORMATION

ADDRESS: 51 San Martín St. Ph. 02323 42-1070.

HOURS: The basilica is open every day from 7 AM to 8 PM. The historical exhibition is open Tuesday to Sunday from 10 AM to 12 PM and 2 PM to 6 PM.

GUIDED TOURS: To have information about regular guided tours and educational tours, the visitor should contact telephone (02323) 43-5101.

FACTS

POPE JOHN PAUL II VISIT

The pope celebrated a mass in front of the Luján Basilica for 600 thousand people on June 11, 1982.

THE STAINED GLASS works from 19th Century constitute one of the largest collections in Argentina.

59

THE MAIN NAVE is 97 m (318 ft) in length and 30 m (98 ft) in height.

THE PRIESTS' DWELLINGS are located in the central garden area.

THE MUSEUM exhibits a replica of the Luján Virgin wearing the original mantle with a escutcheon from 1930.

THE VIRGIN'S CROWN containing 365 precious stones was blessed by Pope Leon XIII.

THE EXHIBITION displays the historical and religious evolution of Luján including Father Salvaire history. The distinction granted by Pope John Paul II during his visit is exhibited between a gold tabernacle and precious stones.

San Antonio de Areco and Surroundings

The second sector of this itinerary is located on the northwest part of Buenos Aires, 112 kilometers from the city. Since the times where posts and small fortress were in the area, the population is considered one of the most traditional in the entire province. The rural scenery was depicted in Ricardo Güiraldes novel, *Don Segundo Sombra*.

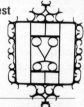

❶ SAN ANTONIO DE ARECO ✱✱✱

Places of interest:

● Museo Gasparini
● Centro Cultural and Museo Usina Vieja
● Museo Gauchesco Ricardo Güiraldes
● Puente Viejo

● Museo Gauchesco Ricardo Güiraldes *(San Antonio de Areco)* pays homage to the writer.

● Puente Viejo *(San Antonio de Areco)* was inaugurated on May 4, 1857 to communicate people living on both sides of Areco river.

● Museo Gasparini *(San Antonio de Areco)* is a cottage in memory of Osvaldo Gasparini.

● Centro Cultural and Museo Usina Vieja *(S.A. Areco)* exhibits works of local artists.

✱ SIGHTS TO SEE

- **SAN ANTONIO DE ARECO**
- **ESTANCIA LA CINACINA**
- **ESTANCIA LA PORTEÑA**
- **ESTANCIA EL OMBU DE ARECO**

FIRST LUXURY EDITION

In 1929, three years after the first edition of *Don Segundo Sombra*, a luxury edition of Güiraldes' book was printed in Holland.

⑤ ESTANCIA LA BAMBA ✳✳

The colonial house where coaches changed horses in former times has 6 hectares, an observatory roofed galleries and a patio with a cistern.

❸ ESTANCIA LA PORTEÑA ✳✳✳

Don Segundo Sombra *author, Ricardo Güiraldes lived here.*

61

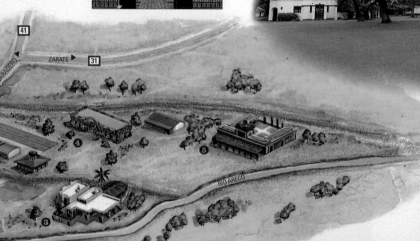

41
BARADERO
ZARATE ▶ 31
RIO ARECO

❷ ESTANCIA LA CINACINA ✳✳✳

It has a museum devoted to the activities in the Argentine countryside.

❹ ESTANCIA EL OMBU DE ARECO ✳✳✳

Oaks, eucalyptus, araucaria and the traditional ombú are planted on the estancia's 300 hectares.

0km		3
0miles		2

This sector starts in San Antonio de Areco a city located 112 kilometers from Buenos Aires.

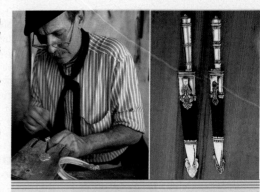

SAN ANTONIO DE ARECO | 1

Founded on October 23, 1730 by José Ruiz de Arellano, the origin of the name is attributed to different facts with two versions. First version says that the name comes from of the areca plant growing at the shore of the river; the plant was used by Amerindians to prepare *buyo* a paste to chew. The second version talks about an Spanish official named Areco who fought against the Amerindians. As a matter of fact, the names of the areas are generally more related to facts than to an almost nonexistent colonial tradition.

THE ARECO'S ARTISANS

The first exposition of crafts in San Antonio de Areco was held in 1936. Since 1971 the Day of the Tradition is celebrated in Areco town. During the whole week, artisans take a preponderant place in the town and their crafts are exhibited during the popular celebration.

However, the workshops are open all year round in the urban center of Areco. The excellent crafts developed in the area include rope artisanship, gaucho's silver works, weaving, colonial carpentry and boot manufacture.

MUSEO GASPARINI

Gasparini Museum Facade.

Gasparini Museum. Drawer Luis Gasparini built an adobe hut with French tiles supported by palm trees in honor to his father Osvaldo Gasparini who was born Laboulaye, Córdoba Province. This autodidact artist lived with gaucho Segundo Ramírez; this character who was source of inspiration for Ricardo Güiraldes in his masterwork. Gasparini's

paintings decorate San Antonio de Padua church and houses in Areco. Inside of the museum, three halls are devoted to the painter's work. In the backyard there is a small chapel and a sculpture representing an Amerindian family from the Areco area. The most well-known work by Gasparini is the *Martín Fierro* edition in Braille system.
III ALVEAR AND BOLIVAR STREET.

CENTRO CULTURAL AND MUSEO USINA VIEJA ②

Cultural Center and Usina Vieja Museum. Created in 1992 on the grounds where the first power plant of Areco town functioned. The place is used by local artists to exhibit their works; among the exhibited objects is the first plane used by a resident of the area; there is also a hall devoted

The first plane used for an Areco inhabitant in the Usina Vieja Museum.

DAY OF THE TRADITION

Since 1939, every year on November 10 the Day of Tradition has been celebrated to commemorate the anniversary of the birth of Jose Hernández; in the Criollo Park the celebration offers among other things shows of horsemen's skills and troops of horses in an unusual parade.

Main house, Criollo Park and Gaucho Museum Ricardo Güiraldes.

to Areco's artisans and old agricultural machinery. The museum is devoted to exhibitions of paintings, photographs and sculptures of local artists.

III 66 ALSINA STREET. HOURS MONDAY THROUGH FRIDAY 9 AM TO 5 PM. SATURDAY AND SUNDAY FROM 10 AM TO 5 PM.

MUSEO GAUCHESCO RICARDO GÜIRALDES

Ricardo Güiraldes Gaucho Museum. Inaugurated October 16, 1938 Ricardo Güiraldes Gaucho Museum exhibits representations of the Argentine past related to the gaucho, his customs, way of living and his contribution to the country. At the entrance of the large park is the Pulpería La Blanqueada reproducing a grocery store and restaurant of that time. The pulperia shows a counter with bars where unknown customers were served and an enclosed room where the owner admitted only regular customers. Located opposite the Pulpería is the hermitage, a small sanctuary with a 17th Century image of the town saint patron, San Antonio de Padua. In the main house, there are different halls dedicated to the estancia's owner

rooms, to the writers, to the gaucho and to the personality and literary work of famous writer Ricardo Güiraldes.

III CAMINO RICARDO GÜIRALDES. HOURS: WEDNESDAY TO MONDAY FROM 11 AM TO 5 PM.

PUENTE VIEJO

Sight of the Old Bridge.

The old bridge was made of bricks and with only one arch during 1857. Since the first of January of 1858 a toll was charged for its maintenance because the bridge was used by the people living on both shores of Areco river at the north of the town. Today, cars are not allowed in order to preserve the old appearance. ●

III MORENO AND ARECO RIVER.

A WRITER OF THE COUNTRYSIDE

Argentine writer Ricardo Güiraldes was born in 1886. He spent his life in the city and in the estancia La Porteña de Areco. In the latter he was inspired to write his masterpiece and well acclaimed book Don Segundo Sombra published June 1st 1926.

○ *Leaving the old bridge, the visitor will go along Moreno two blocks to Lavalle Street, on the right side is La Cinacina Estancia.*

ESTANCIA LA CINACINA | 2

La Cinacina Ranch. On the grounds of the estancia are a hermitage, a carriage shed and a museum with seven halls exhibiting significant tools, utensils and ornaments related to the agricultural activity in the Argentine countryside. It is an ideal place to spend a day in the country and enjoy a show of traditional music and dance accompanied by delicious home made dishes. Races for a ringlet, special horse races called *cuadreras* and horse troops are shown on the premises. The visitor may ride sulkies and witness the tame of horse; all these activities may allow the visitor to have a precise idea of the real life and rites of Pampean *gaucho*.

▓ 9 BARTOLOME MITRE. PHONE 45-2773.

▶ *Along Mitre Street to Route 8, then turn left until arriving at Route 41, five kilometers ahead the visitor will arrive to the path leading to La Porteña.*

Pulpería in La Cinacina Estancia.

Sight of the inside of the large house in La Cinacina Estancia, today is a Museum.

ESTANCIA LA PORTEÑA | 3

La Porteña Main House.

La Porteña Ranch. In the middle of an old park designed by architect and landscaper Carlos Thays is the legendary estancia La Porteña. Three leagues from the urban part of San Antonio de Areco, it was the residence of writer and poet Ricardo Güiraldes, creator of gaucho novel *Don Segundo Sombra* of great importance for the Argentine people; therefore the site is linked to literature. It was one of the first estancias in the country to favor rural tourism offering lodging for a day or a weekend.

◆ MORE INFORMATION ON PAGE 66-67.

LA PULPERIA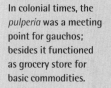

In colonial times, the *pulpería* was a meeting point for gauchos; besides it functioned as grocery store for basic commodities.

▶ *Leaving La Porteña, the visitor will come back to Route 41 towards Baradero until reaching Route 31 to turn right again and 5 kilometers ahead is El Ombú.*

ESTANCIA EL OMBU DE ARECO | 4

El Ombú de Areco Ranch has three hundred hectares and is named after the most typical tree in the Plains, the umbra tree *(ombú).* In 1890 Pablo Ricchieri built the main part of the estancia, his Italian origin is evidenced in the architectural style chosen at the end of 19th Century. Subsequently, Enrique Boelcke bought the house in 1934. Alberto Viaggio is the husband of the present owner who opened the estancia to the tourists. Located 120 kilometers from Buenos Aires, the four hectares park is planted with palms, eucalyptus and casuarina trees. The facilities include nine bedrooms with private bath renovated keeping the colonial style. The visitor may spend one or several days, ride one of the thirty-eight horses or wander around the estancia in sulky. El Ombú de Areco facilities also include a large swimming pool, a solarium, billiard tables, a soccer field, volley court and table play games.

||| ROUTE 31 TO ZARATE 4TH QUARTERS. INFORMATION PHONE (02326)49 2080.

Entrance to the Main Part of El Ombú de Areco Estancia.

► *Leaving El Ombú de Areco Estancia, the visitor will go back to Route 31 towards Zárate, 3 Km ahead is La Bamba Estancia.*

where voyagers stopped to rest and horses were changed. The construction was made in 1932;

ESTANCIA LA BAMBA | 5

La Bamba Ranch is a traditional estancia in the area that still carries out agricultural and cattle raising activities. The architectural style is colonial containing observatories, roofed galleries and a typical patio with the cistern. In the past the main house served as a post for El Camino Real passengers. Camino Real (Royal Road) was the name of the route joining Buenos Aires with the north of the country

La Bamba Estancia Facade.

ATADA DE ARECO
Every year, during the last days of April this celebration called *Atada de los Pagos de Areco* is held in the urban area. From the estancias leave wagons, carriages and horses to make exhibitions of skills and games.

its sixteen hectares are prepared to receive tourists who can ride horses, drive a wagon, fish and enjoy shows of folkloric dances and horseman's skills. ∎

||| ROUTE 31 TO ZARATE, IN THE CROSSING OF ROUTE 8 AND ROUTE 41 (KM 110). INFORMATION BY TELEPHONE (02236) 45-6293.

THE ORIGEN OF THE ESTANCIAS

Large estancias like La Porteña (on the right) were lands occupied by the Amerindians conquered by military personnel. At the beginning, most landowners were military personnel who started profitable activities in the countryside.

Estancia La Porteña

La Porteña Ranch. Located 120 kilometers from Buenos Aires in San Antonio de Areco, it was named after the first Argentine locomotive. Since 1912, writer Ricardo Güiraldes and his family lived in this estancia; he was inspired in the landscape and characters of the area to write his novel *Don Segundo Sombra*.

A
RICARDO GÜIRALDES
EN EL CENTENARIO DE SU NACIMIENTO
1886-13 de Febrero-1986
EN EL LUGAR DE LA CREACIÓN DE SU OBRA
ASOCIACIÓN DE AMIGOS DEL PARQUE CRIOLLO Y
MUSEO GAUCHESCO RICARDO GÜIRALDES

THE GALLERY
This external space, very common in the estancias is used to receive guests.

SPECIAL ENTRANCE
Waiting room for visitors.

STYLISH PARK
Carlos Thays, creator of many important parks in the country, designed the park around the estancia.

FORMER ENTRANCE
There are imposing oak trees planted in the path leading to the main house.

66

ClarinX

USEFUL INFORMATION

ADDRESS: 5 kilometers from RP 41 and 6 kilometers from crossing RP 41 and RN 8. Telephone (02326) 45-3770.

VISITS: Open every day fro, 8:30 AM. Reservations in advance by telephone.

FACILITIES The estancia has comfortable facilities to lodge tourists who may spend a day or a weekend.

FACTS

LEBANESE CEDAR TREE
Ricardo Güiraldes used to rest under this tree when writing his novel *Don Segundo Sombra.*

RICARDO GÜIRALDES' LIBRARY

Ricardo Güiraldes wrote his novel *Don Segundo Sombra* on this room located on the second floor. Today, the estancia's guests may spend a night there.

67

PART OF THE MAIN HOUSE *was built in 19th Century and today is surrounded by a centennial park.*

POLO FIELD. *The sport may be practiced under the owners' supervision.*

The Gauchos' Road

In the rural area of the west side of Buenos Aires, customs related to the *gauchos* are still present in their daily life such as garments, horse riding, barbecue and mate by the campfire.

Beef for Exportation

Juan de Garay brought cattle in 1580. In the 19th Century some breeding animals were imported to improve the quality of the animals. A wire fence was set on the terrain to favor the crossing, selection and half-breed.

Hereford

Shorthorn

Holando Argentino

Aberdeen Angus

Different ways of carving

In the drawing *(right)* different kinds of traditional meat cuts used in the Argentine cuisine.

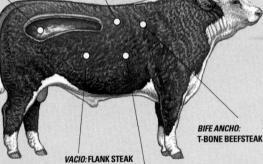

LOMO: BEEFSTEAK (BONELESS MEAT)

BIFE ANGOSTO: SIRLOIN STEAK

BIFE ANCHO: T-BONE BEEFSTEAK

VACIO: FLANK STEAK

ASADO: ROAST RIBS

The *Asado Criollo*

The secret in the recipe is to maintain the fire in the adequate proportion and cook the meat gradually. There a different ways of cooking the meat: in a spit or grill with or without the skin.

GAUCHO'S ATTIRE

Gauchos in the countryside usually wear a jackknife and belt with silver coins, the former is an instrument for personal protection and also used in rural chores. The use of the belt with silver coins began in the times when they carried money attached to the belt.

The Mate's Circle

Silver Work Mates.

◄ The mate is an infusion drank in a container called also mate with a metal straw offered as an expression of courtesy and fraternity. Originally the mate and the straw were made of plants, today they are made of different materials covered with elaborate leather of silver works.

Traditional Skills

Ancestral rural activities have become games, sports and competitions that enliven gauchos' celebrations; among them, the tame of horses, special horse races called *cuadreras* and races for a ringlet are noteworthy.

Sortija

◄ a Races for a Ringlet. While galloping, a horseman tries to put a stick in a metallic hoop hanging from a crosspiece.

Doma

▲ Time of a Horse. Originally used in the countryside tasks, it is the skill of domesticating a wild horse with strength and dexterity.

Linked Lagoons

De Lobos, San Miguel del Monte and Chascomus lagoons resemble huge mirrors in the middle of the Pampa surrounded by the greenery and serenity of the area, they offer all possibilities for lacustrine leisure.

PLAZA DE CHASCOMUS

IGLESIA SAN MIGUEL ARCANGEL

FOUNTAIN IN ESTANCIA SAN MARTIN

MUNICIPALIDAD DE CHASCOMUS

LAGUNA DE CHASCOMUS

LAGUNA DE LOBOS

WINDSURF IN CHASCOMUS

CHASCOMUS CHURCH

CATTLE IN CAÑUELAS COUNTRYSIDE

JUAN MANUEL DE ROSAS RANCH

ESTANCIA SAN MARTIN CHAPEL IN CAÑUELAS

ARROYO VITEL

From Lobos to Chascomús

The itinerary consists of three sectors. Each one of them situated around one of the three lacustrine systems known as Lagunas Encadenadas. The first one wanders around Laguna de Lobos, the second one around Laguna del Monte and the last one around Laguna de Chascomús. The whole area is rich in historical references with a particular attraction: the array of estancias where the visitor will experience the Pampean rural life.

Sector 1
LOBOS AND SURROUNDINGS

SIGHTS TO SEE

❶ Lobos ✳✳✳ : Plaza 1810, Iglesia del Carmen, Museo and Biblioteca Juan D. Perón, Parque Municipal Hiriart ❷ Aeroclub Fortín de Lobos ✳✳✳ ❸ Laguna de Lobos ✳✳✳ ❹ Estancia La Candelaria ✳✳✳✳ ❺ Estancia Santa Rita ✳✳✳ ❻ Cañuelas ✳✳ ❼ Estancia La Martina ✳✳✳ ❽ Estancia El Metejón ✳✳

SOME TIPS
To fully experience the activities at the estancia, it is advisable to program a whole day, or even better a weekend.

TIME TO ALLOT

❚❚ **The visit** will take a day.
▶ **A rapid visit** half a day.

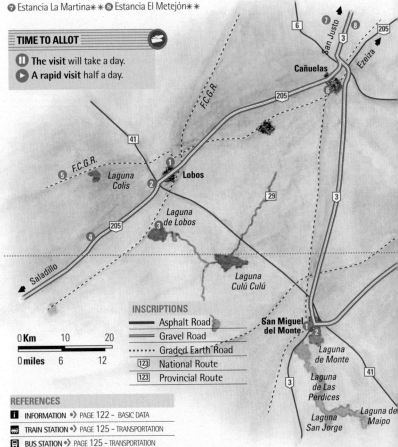

INSCRIPTIONS

———	Asphalt Road
═══	Gravel Road
······	Graded Earth Road
123	National Route
123	Provincial Route

0 Km   10   20
0 miles   6   12

REFERENCES

ℹ️ INFORMATION •▷ PAGE 122 – BASIC DATA
🚂 TRAIN STATION •▷ PAGE 125 – TRANSPORTATION
🚌 BUS STATION •▷ PAGE 125 – TRANSPORTATION
✈️ AIRPORT ▷ PAGE 125 – TRANSPORTATION

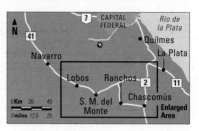

TIME TO ALLOT	Detailed Visit: 3 days.
	Rapid Visit: 1 day and a half.
DISTANCE	250 km approx. (155 miles).
MEANS	By car and on foot.

Sector 2
SAN MIGUEL DEL MONTE

SIGHTS TO SEE
❶ San Miguel del Monte ✳✳✳: Iglesia de San Miguel Arcángel, Plaza Alsina, Rancho de Rosas
❷ Laguna de Monte ✳✳✳ ❸ Brandsen ✳✳

SOME TIPS
In order to catch *pejerrey* (a variety of mackerel) in the lagoons it is advisable to use lightweight spear because this fish is very challenging to catch.

73

TIME TO ALLOT
❚❚ **A detailed visit** to the sector will take a whole day.
▶ **Visiting quickly** the main points of the sector will take half a day.

Sector 3
CHASCOMUS AND SURROUNDINGS

SIGHTS TO SEE
❶ Chascomús ✳✳✳: Catedral de la Merced, Casa de Casco, Palacio Municipal, Teatro Brazzola, Museo Pampeano ❷ Fuerte de San Juan Bautista ✳✳ ❸ Laguna de Chascomús ✳✳✳✳ ❹ Estancia La Fe ✳✳✳ ❺ Estancia La Horqueta ✳✳✳ ❻ Estancia La Mamaia ✳✳

TIME TO ALLOT
❚❚ **To visit** the sector at a relaxed pace will take a whole day.
▶ **To visit** the most important points of interest will take half a day.

Lobos and Surroundings

The cities of Lobos and Cañuelas are located to the southeast of the city of Buenos Aires in a plain landscape surrounded by numerous lagoons suitable for fishing. The sector also offers plenty of estancias where the visitor will be able to participate in local sports; polo may be learned or practiced in the area.

❸ LAGUNA DE LOBOS ✳✳✳

The lagoon located near the city of the same name is visited by a great number of sportive fishermen. Every summer there is a local celebration.

❷ AEROCLUB FORTIN DE LOBOS ✳✳✳

Apart from the activities related to aviation, there are many sports facilities.

○ The city was founded Where Del Carmen church is located *(Lobos).*

❶ LOBOS ✳✳✳

Places of interest:

○ Plaza 1810
○ Iglesia del Carmen
○ Museo y Biblioteca Perón
○ Parque Municipal

○ Juan D. Perón Museum and Library maintains memorabilia belonging to the former president.

0km	5
0miles	3

SIGHTS TO SEE

- **LOBOS**

- **LAGUNA DE LOBOS**

- **ESTANCIA LA CANDELARIA**

- **ESTANCIA SANTA RITA**

FACTS

JUAN MOREIRA
In one of the halls in Juan D. Perón Museum there is an exhibition of objects belonging to the famous gaucho Juan Moreira murdered in Lobos; his skull is exhibited with a peculiar catapult.

④ ESTANCIA LA CANDELARIA ✶✶✶✶
Carlos Thays designed the spacious park.

❼ ESTANCIA LA MARTINA ✶✶
The estancia known for polo activities contains all amenities for the practice of this equestrian sport.

75

SALVADOR MARIA
The town is named in memory former Vice President Salvador María del Carril. He used to own of the grounds where the town is located.

❻ CAÑUELAS ✶✶
This town has been a diary products traditional center.

❽ ESTANCIA EL METEJON ✶✶
This modern estancia is opened to the public and its facilities are devoted to polo practice and instruction.

❺ ESTANCIA SANTA RITA ✶✶✶
An historical establishment renovated in the 90s for lodging tourists.

The itinerary starts in the urban area of Lobos, 100 km (62 miles) at the southwest of the Federal Capital. It is a rural and plain area surrounded by lagoons.

LOBOS | 1

On August 21, 1779, the artillery sergeant Pedro Rodriguez finished the main parts of San Pedro de los Lobos Fort located at the shore of the lagoon. The Viceroy granted Don José Salgado some lands two leagues at the north of the Fort at the end of 18th Century where he built a chapel in 1802. The chapel was inaugurated in 1803 and Lobos town developed moderately around it.

PLAZA 1810

1810 Square. The main plaza 1810 is located opposite Del Carmen Church, the grounds were granted by Don Manuel Antonio Caminos, the first Judge of the jurisdiction. In the beginning, it was Buenos Aires by name for being the route from and towards the Capital; the name lasted until the centenary of the Independence when it became 1810 Plaza.

NUTRIAS AND DOGS
The nutrias at the shore were called river wolfs or water wolfs, therefore the name of the place. Another story says that the name is due to the savage dogs in the vicinity of the lagoon.

IGLESIA NUESTRA SEÑORA DEL CARMEN ②

Lobos Main Church.

Nuestra Señora del Carmen Church is a symbol of the city's foundation. Located at the same place where the first chapel was erected in 1802, the first houses were built around it. The first neighbor was José Salgado and his family, and the 141 inhabitants who at that time lived in the different farms in the area.

MUSEO Y BIBLIOTECA ③ JUAN D. PERON

Museum and Library Juan D. Perón. The building preserves the architectural style of the end of 19th Century and the beginning of 20th Century. The Museum was created October 25, 1953 and closed during the military government in 1955. Until its reopening in 1973, some of its objects were exhibited in Lobos Municipality. In 1976, the military government closed it once again. Finally, Buenos Aires Governor Antonio Cafiero reopened the Museum on July 1st 1989. Today, it exhibits Perón's furniture and personal belongings. The 25 de Octubre hall in the museum exhibits an important photographic collection showing the former president visiting his hometown.

▌▌▌ 482 JUAN DOMINGO PERON ST. PHONE (02227) 42-3110. VISITING HOURS: WED THROUGH SUN FROM 10 AM TO 12 AM AND FROM 3 PM TO 6 PM

Peron's Bed Exhibited in the Museum.

PARQUE MUNICIPAL ④ INGENIERO HIRIART

Engineer Hiriart Municipal Park. Designed in 1918, it has 17 hectares with trees and recreational areas. The park has a soccer field, where matches organized by the Liga Lobense are played and sport facilities complex for practicing athletics, volleyball and basketball.

▌▌▌ SALGADO AND INDEPENDENCIA ST. HOURS: MON THROUGH SUN 7 AM TO 8 PM.

1810 Plaza, Located Opposite Lobos Municipality.

Sight of Fermín Villarruel Sport Complex.

▶ Along Salgado St turning right on Junin St, a block ahead the visitor will turn right on San Martín St and once again right on Perón Av. When arriving at Route 205, the visitor will turn right up to Km 105 to arrive at Aeroclub.

AEROCLUB FORTIN DE LOBOS | 2

Parachuting in Lobos District.

The Aeroclub Fortín de Lobos on 100 hectares (247 acres) terrain was inaugurated in 1959 and devoted to aviation activities. In 1973, other sports were added and a golf course, a swimming pool and recreational facilities were built. Rugby, soccer and volleyball courts are the newest additions. The golf court, approved by the Argentine Golf Association, has 18 holes. A parachuting school, pilots training school and an area for the construction of model airplanes functions here as well. The institution has a landing field for night and day flights.

JESUITS CROSS

In 1872 the Catholic Jesuit-ical Mission arrived in Lobos. From that time, there remain some wooden crosses with brick pedestals located at the north of the town at the shore of Salgado channel. A similar one was erected in Perón Street in the south area of the town.

▌ 205 ROUTE, KM. 105.5 PHONE: (02227) 421700. HOURS: GOLF: TUE THROUGH SUN AND HOLIDAYS. PARACHUTING AND TANDEM: ADVANCED RESERVATION PHONE 4962-9988.

▶ *Leaving the Fortin the Lobos, the visitor will return to Route 205 to the right side until reaching Kilometer 115, then turn left to arrive at Lobos Lagoon.*

LAGUNA DE LOBOS | 3

Lobos Lagoon. The fresh water lagoon located 15 kilometers from the town with a surface of 800 hectares (1,975 acres) ideal for water sports constitutes the main attraction of the area. Due to the abundant vegetation, there are a great variety of birds. The ichthyological fauna is mainly composed of pejerreyes (mackerel variety), carps, tarariras (Argentine fresh water fish), breams and striped mullets. During December and January, the Sports Fishermen Gathering is celebrated and the event is considered of tourist interest. During the gathering, different competitions related to water sports are held and the Sports Fishermen Queen is elected while musicians play on an aquatic stage; Lobos Fishermen Club founded in 1945 organizes the event. The club has many boats, a dock 150 m (492 ft) in length, a restaurant and store for supplies. In the lagoon, there are camping areas, clubs, stores and restaurants. ↻

↝ MORE INFORMATION ON PAGE 92-93.

77

Lobos Lagoon located 115 kilometers from Buenos Aires.

○ *Returning to Route 205, the visitor will turn left 2 km (1.24 miles) to arrive at La Candelaria.*

ESTANCIA LA CANDELARIA | 4

Particular Tower in Santa Rita Estancia, added by today owners.

Historical Main House from 16th Century.

La Candelaria Ranch is located on 100 hectares (247 acres) terrain. The castle, designed by French Alberto Fabre, has three stories containing a sitting room, dinner rooms, game rooms, bedrooms and a library. Landscaper architect Carlos Thays designed the park. The rest of the accommodations in colonial style are located around the spacious park containing more than 240 types of trees.

‖‖ ROUTE 205, KM 114.5.

▶ *Going along Route 205 towards Lobos until reaching Route 41 crossing, the visitor will turn left and continue 7 km (4,3 mi) ahead, there, he will turn left 20 km (12 mi) to arrive at Santa Rita Estancia.*

ESTANCIA SANTA RITA | 5

Santa Rita Ranch. In the second half of 18th Century, Buenos Aires was threatened by the Amerindian's invasions. Along the Salado river forts were created to protect inhabitant from the attacks; behind the fortress some dwellings and a chapel were erected. These constructions are the antecedent of the first estancias in Buenos Aires province. An example of these constructions is Santa Rita Estancia, recycled and modernized in 1996 to lodge tourists. A 40 hectares (99 acres) centennial forest surrounds the main historical house in the style of European residences in colonial times when the house belonged to Juan Manuel de Rosas' relatives.

‖‖ LOCATED 2 KM (1.2 MI) FROM CARBONI STATION. TELEPHONE (02227) 49 5026.

ESTANCIA LA FIGURA ◉
Located in Uribelarrea town, this establishment belonged to Engineer Carlos E. Pellegrini who devised Buenos Aires Port.

▶ *Returning to Route 41 until crossing Route 205, the visitor will turn left and 38 kilometers ahead is Cañuelas.*

ESTANCIA SAN MARTIN

Vicente L Casares was only 18 years old when he founded San Martin Estancia in Cañuelas in 1866. He was convinced of the future of the diary product industry when he founded La Martona, the first diary product firm in the country in 1886. Carlos Thays designed the park.

CAÑUELAS 6

Cañuelas town was founded January 22, 1822. In La Caledonia Estancia, the Cañuelas Treaty was signed on June 24, 1829 establishing pacification between Juan Manuel de Rosas and Juan Lavalle. Cañuelas area is famous for starting the diary industry in the country. La Martona started business in San Martín Estancia and the first exports of wheat to Europe were accomplished in the country. Besides, the first wire-entanglement in an establishment of this kind was set. The town, first El Carmen en las Cañuelas and later, El Carmen de Cañuelas was named after a local plant called *espaldaña*, a one meter in height gramineous plant with wide and pointed leaves. Several historical events took place in the area like the establishment a frontier to avoid Amerindians invasions.

▶ *Returning to Route 205, the visitor will turn left until reaching the round. Along Route 3 towards Almirante Brown exit, on the left is La Martina.*

ESTANCIA LA MARTINA 7

La Martina Ranch. Located in Vicente Casares, 50 kilometers from Buenos Aires, the estancia is famous for its facilities devoted to the polo sport. Besides polo, other sports may be practiced; there are tennis, paddle and volleyball courts, a swimming pool and carts. During high season conspicuous polo players take part in activities in the estancia, however, the facilities are open all year round. It has three houses and a house club with 25 rooms,

Sight of the main plaza in Cañuelas, located opposite the church.

LA CALEDONIA

This estancia, located in Carmen de Cañuelas district and founded by John Miller in 1823 has plenty of authentic rural settings belonging to the first part of 19th Century.

16 of them are suites and a 160 sq m (191 sq yd) hall prepared to host conventions and parties. In La Martinta Polo Ranch, the visitor may spend a country day or weekend. Beginners are guided by instructors and trained in a wooden horse.

Ⅲ ALMIRANTE BROWN AVENUE NO NUMBER. VICENTE CASARES. TELEPHONE (02226) 43-0777.

Polo Horses in La Martina.

▶ *Going along Almirante Brown Street, the visitor will cross Route 3, on the right side is El Metejón Estancia.*

ESTANCIA EL METEJON 8

Sitting Room in El Metejón

El Metejón Ranch. El Metejón Polo Ranch is located in Vicente Casares district. Surrounded by a verdant environment, the visitor will find polo courts with first class instructors and players. The estancia has 6 suites in the house club and 5 rooms in the main house. It also has two large rooms for 60 and 100 people respectively for conventions and parties and a soccer field. Company meetings and country days for families are organized on the premises. ■

Ⅲ ALMIRANTE BROWN AVENUE AND SIEMPRE VIVA STREET. VICENTE CASARES. TELEPHONE (02226) 43-2260

San Miguel del Monte

Monte Lagoon surroundings combine historical sights with a natural environment for recreational activities, fishing and water sports. These lands witnessed the first advanced guards against the Amerindians in the military campaign Campaña del Desierto. Rural life habits may be witnessed here.

❶ SAN MIGUEL DEL MONTE ✳✳✳

Places of interest:

◉ Iglesia San Miguel Arcángel
◉ Plaza Adolfo Alsina
◉ Rancho de Rosas

◉ Iglesia San Miguel Arcángel *(San Miguel del Monte).* Well-known Argentine artists decorated the interior.

◉ Plaza Adolfo Alsina *(San Miguel del Monte).*

41

3

❷ LAGUNA DE MONTE ✳✳✳

The north coast offers a great variety of gastronomical recreational and tourist services while the south coast keeps its bucolic beauty.

✳ SIGHTS TO SEE

- **IGLESIA SAN MIGUEL ARCANGEL**
- **RANCHO DE ROSAS**
- **LAGUNA DE MONTE**
- **BRANDSEN**

FACTS

LOS CERRILLOS
Juan Manuel de Rosas'
estancia near Monte
where Rosas created
a militia called
Los Colorados
del Monte.

FISHING SEASON CLOSES
Fishing season closes between
October 1st and November 30
in Monte Lagoon, the restric-
tion is imposed in order to
preserve the local Pejerrey.

81

❸ BRANDSEN ✳✳
*In the first half of 18ᵗʰ Century Brandsen was established
as a settlement in the area around the El Zanjón Fort.
The area became a city after the railway joining
Chascomús and Buenos Aires was inaugurated.*

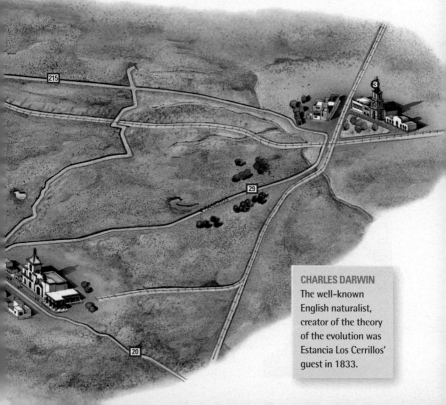

CHARLES DARWIN
The well-known
English naturalist,
creator of the theory
of the evolution was
Estancia Los Cerrillos'
guest in 1833.

This second sector starts in the area of San Miguel del Monte in Buenos Aires province, located 110 kilometers (68 miles) from the southwest of the city.

Sight of the Main Church in San Miguel del Monte.

SAN MIGUEL DEL MONTE

On November 18, 1779, the city of San Miguel de Monte including different provincial jurisdictions was originated in a settlement around a military fort erected by Commander at the frontier Juan José Sarden. Afterwards, San Miguel del Monte Gárgano chapel was erected and the urban population gathered around the chapel dedicated to the saint San Miguel del Monte Gárgano. Until 1780, these lands were part of La Matanza area. Narrow streets with colonial corners, old houses with iron wrought fences protecting their gardens still remain; there are also the typical straw shacks. In the south of the city at the shore of Monte lagoon, modern build-ings and a renovated avenue by the coast is visible. The area has polo, fishing, hunting, nautical and boating clubs, recreational and camping areas and bathing areas.

OLD FORT

Located in the area between Vértiz Plaza and the lagoon, these grounds were considered the most important defense part of the frontier constantly threatened by the Amerindians invasion.

IGLESIA SAN MIGUEL ARCANGEL

San Miguel Arcángel Church. Inaugurated in 1867, this church is related to many important events in the past. The church was reconstructed four times; the present building has a plain appearance and a large tower

PLAZA ESPAÑA

España Square *Located in the center of the urban area of San Miguel del Monte, the plaza is surrounded by houses of the era. In the middle of the plaza there is the sculptured bust of Juan Manuel de Rosas who acquired the Los Cerrillos Estancia after the May Revolution.*

and a belfry donated by Juan Cappizzano in 1890. The parochial house keeps the Monte Infantry Battalion of the National Guard first flag; the battalion was created between 1882 and 1884. Paintings by artists such as Horacio Butler, Ernesto de la Cárcova, Héctor Basaldúa, Ester Barugel and Raúl Soldi decorate the interior of the church. The neoclassic style facade has a central tower; on one side the oldness of the construction can be appreciated.

III H. YRIGOYEN AND BARTOLOME MITRE STREET (CORNER).

PLAZA ADOLFO ALSINA

Opposite San Miguel Arcángel Church is the main plaza Adolfo Alsina located on Petrachi, Bartolomé Mitre, H. Yrigoyen and L N. Alem streets where the town's people usually gather. Opposite, the Municipality is noticeable; half a block along Petrachi Street is Enrique Uzal Cultural Center where temporal exhibitions by local artist are presented. The Municipal Popular Library contains books and historical documents depicting the way of life of this jurisdiction of the Buenos Aires province.

PATO FILLOL

The national soccer team goalkeeper during 1978 World Cup, Ubaldo Matildo Fillol (Pato) was born and lived until he was 14 years old in the city of San Miguel del Monte.

Aldofo Alsina Plaza. Located opposite Monte Municipality.

RANCHO DE ROSAS ③

Rosas' Ranch. Originally located in Estancia Los Cerrillos, in 1987 the Bemberg family, the present owners, relocated Governor Juan Manuel de Rosas' ranch in the urban center.

▐ SOLER AND BELGRANO STREET. HOURS: SATURDAY, SUNDAY AND HOLIDAYS FROM 10 AM TO 12:30 AM AND FROM 3 PM TO 5:30 PM.

Facade of the Ranch owned by Rosas.

▶ *Leaving Rosas' Ranch, the visitor will turn right on Belgrano Street and continue along a block until arriving at the lagoon.*

LAGUNA DE MONTE ②

Monte Lagoon. This extensive lagoon has a surface of 740 hectares (1,827 acres) and a maximum depth of 2 meters (6.6 ft). It is the ideal place for practicing water sports such as water-skiing, windsurf, sailing, canoeing, kayaking and floating bicycles. Many tourists and locals find in this peaceful environment a rewarding rest from the city. The coast presents two different areas, the north area with parks offers tourist services, hotels, restaurants and discos. The south area keeps the bucolic beauty with plenty of trees and a great variety of birds.

•▶ MORE INFORMATION ON PAGE 92-93.

▶ *Leaving the lagoon and going along Belgrano Street until reaching Blandengues, the visitor will turn right towards Route 215, along the route 61 km. ahead (38 miles) is Coronel Brandsen.*

BRANDSEN ③

Brandsen Church Facade.

The first inhabitants of this town were residents of El Zanjón Fort during the first half of 18th Century. The present city, located in the neighboring area of Ferrari railway station was constituted by a group of dwellings built on a portion of land granted by Pedro José Ferrari on October 9, 1865. Ferrari was the first judge and founder of Coronel Brandsen jurisdiction. ∎

▐ ROUTE 215 AND ROUTE 29.

The lagoon is the main attraction in San Miguel del Monte.

83

Chascomús and Surroundings

The system of linked lagoons is located to the south-west of Buenos Aires city. From the seven lagoons, Chascomús is the largest. The city by the samename located at the shore of the lagoon and the estancias in the surrounding area constitute an interesting tourist spot.

❺ ESTANCIA LA HORQUETA ✳✳✳

Located 5 kilometers from Chascomús beside Viten lagoon, it has a 6 hectares (15 acres) park with trees of different species.

❸ LAGUNA DE CHASCOMUS ✳✳✳✳

One of the seven linked lagoons is the main attraction.

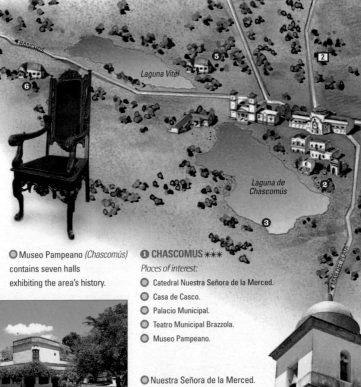

Laguna Vitel

Laguna de Chascomús

⬤ Museo Pampeano *(Chascomús)* contains seven halls exhibiting the area's history.

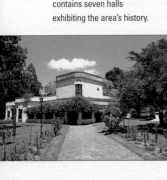

❶ CHASCOMUS ✳✳✳

Places of interest:

⬤ Catedral Nuestra Señora de la Merced.
⬤ Casa de Casco.
⬤ Palacio Municipal.
⬤ Teatro Municipal Brazzola.
⬤ Museo Pampeano.

⬤ Nuestra Señora de la Merced. *(Chascomús)* Inaugurated in 1847, it is located in the highest point and became Cathedral in 1980.

✳ SIGHTS TO SEE

- **LAGUNA DE CHASCOMUS**
- **CHASCOMUS**
- **ESTANCIA LA FE**
- **ESTANCIA LA HORQUETA**

FACTS

PAINTED PHOTOGRAPH
In the Pampean Museum Bartolomé Mitre photograph is noteworthy by the illumination in oil.

❻ ESTANCIA LA MAMAIA ✳✳
Surrounded by parks, the facilities include a swimming pool and playground.

❷ FUERTE DE SAN JUAN BAUTISTA ✳✳
A replica of the city fort erected to protect people from Amerindian invasions. This construction was built on occasion of the celebration of the bicentennial of Chascomús.

❹ ESTANCIA LA FE ✳✳✳
Located 30 km from Chascomus, it has 200 hectares (494 acres) where Samborombón river runs through.

85

MAGDALENA ▶

Laguna Las Mulas

Laguna Yalca

20

❹

⦿ Teatro Municipal Brazzola *(Chascomús)*, founded in 1908.

0km		5
0miles		3

⦿ Palacio Municipal *(Chascomús)*. It is an example of colonial architecture with neoclassic influences.

This last sector starts in Chascomús jurisdiction and is located to the south, 112 kilometers from Buenos Aires near Provincial Route 2.

CHASCOMUS | 1

Viceroy Vertiz ordered Captain Pedro Nicolás Escribano and his troops to found San Juan Bautista Fort on the grounds where today Independencia Plaza is located in the area of Chascomús on May 30, 1779. The first inhabitants were eight Galician families settled in the fort. Afterwards, a group of dwellings gave origin to the present city. Chascomús was the name used by the Amerindians to denominate the lagoon meaning salt water in their own language. Today the city is the most important point of the jurisdiction with thirty thousand inhabitants. The economy has flourished in recent years and is based on cattle raising and some industries located in the area. Tourism is also a source of wealth for the economy of this region. In the recent years many people have visited the parks and comfortable facilities.

RAUL ALFONSIN

Former President Raúl Alfonsín started his political and legislative career in Chascomús town council, located opposite the house where he spent his childhood.

CATEDRAL NUESTRA ①
SEÑORA DE LA MERCED

Nuestra Señora de la Merced Cathedral. In 1832, engineer Felipe Senillosa was commissioned to design the blueprints of a church dedicated to worship San Juan Bautista and Nuestra Señora de la Merced saint patrons of the city. The

De la Merced Cathedral Facade.

church of colonial and plain style was inaugurated on the same location in Chascomús highest point in 1847. In 1980, Pope John Paul II created Chascomús Diocese. Therefore the church became cathedral.

▌▌▌ LAVALLE STREET BETWEEN SARMIENTO AND MITRE STREET. HOURS: EVERY DAY FROM 8 AM TO 9 PM.

CASA DE CASCO ②

Main Corridor in Casco's House.

Casco's House. In 1829, an Amerindians' sudden attack slaughtered the son of the estancia owner Vicente Casco. This sad occurrence impelled the estancia proprietor to order a construction of a more solid

DE LOS NEGROS CHAPEL

In 1860, the black people from Chascomús asked the authorities in the Municipality for a portion of land where today the De los Negros Chapel is located and is one of the points of interest in the area. The construction is very simple, a hut with brick walls, straw roof and a soiled floor. From the original building, *there remain the solid door, some iron windows and a lantern. Throughout the cholera epidemic suffered in the town during the last months of 1866 until the beginning of 1887 the place became a hospital, Imagery and illustrations of black and white saints can be appreciated on the chapel walls.*

house, the first two story house in Chascomús with sun-dried clay brick walls, a brick floor and a balcony. In 1839, in the same house a meeting was held to celebrate the victory of the estancias' owners over Buenos Aires Governor Juan Manuel de Rosas. Subsequently, in 1979 the house was donated to the Municipality. Today the Cultural Department and the Historiography Mu-seum Chascomús y la Cuenca del Salado function on the old premises.

III 43 SARMIENTO STREET. HOURS: MONDAY THROUGH FRIDAY FROM 8 AM TO 7 PM. SUNDAY AND HOLIDAYS FROM 9 AM TO 1 PM AND 3:30 PM TO 5:30 PM.

PALACIO MUNICIPAL ③

Municipal Palace Facade.

Municipal Palace was inaugurated in 1947, architects Francisco Salomé and Piazza y Piana were in charge of the works of this colonial palace with neoclassic influences in the style. The original building was founded in 1856; noteworthy is a large cylinder behind the curved front with eight columns shaped in a lathe. The primitive fort was located on the same place surrounded by sun-dried clay brick houses, a chapel, a *pulpería* and a tree lookout; the only way to enter was through a bridge.

III CRAMER BETWEEN SARMIENTO AND MITRE STREET.

Father Brazzola Municipal Theater.

TEATRO MUNICIPAL ④ BRAZZOLA

Brazzola Municipal Theater. On January 1908, father Julián Quintana founded the Group of Catholic Worker. Father Brazzola support was essential for the group who erected some facilities opposite Independencia Plaza. Engineer Leopoldo Castiella designed the blueprints and the works started on March 1924. Unexpectedly, father Brazzola died and the works stopped until April 24, 1927 when the theater was opened with a modest program: a mass in the church and the ceremony to open the new building. The first performance was not a theatrical representa-

tion but a movie. The theater also functioned as a conference hall for the Workers Group.

III 90 SARMIENTO STREET.

MUSEO PAMPEANO ⑤

Pampean Museum. In 1939, on the occasion of the centenary of Chascomús battle the Museum was created with the support of Governor Manuel Fresco and the Ministry of Public Works, José María Bustillo; Felix Bunge contributed with funds and museum officer and sponsor Enrique Udaondo provided his knowledge of the field. The colonial style of the building was inspired in the Argentine Carrier Post Horse erected in San Isidro. It has seven halls depicting the city and its people's history. ◍

◆) MORE INFORMATION ON PAGE 88-89.

◆) MORE INFORMATION ON PAGE 88-89.

PELOTA CLUB ◉

The Basque community built the social and sportive club located next door to Brazzola Theater in 1925. Very popular sport among Basque people, it is very similar to squash and played with rackets.

De los Libres del Sur Hall in the Pampean Museum.

Museo Pampeano

Pampean Museum. The traditional style house exhibits Chascomús historical patrimony from prehistory to 20th Century. There are fossils from ancient times, objects from the Amerindian culture, gaucho's apparel from the estancias, furniture, daily life objects and important religious works of art.

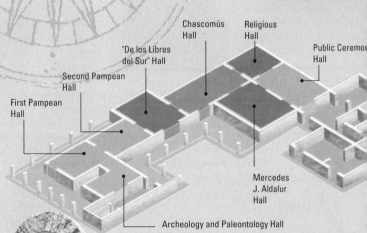

Chascomús Hall

Religious Hall

"De los Libres del Sur" Hall

Public Ceremo Hall

Second Pampean Hall

First Pampean Hall

Mercedes J. Aldalur Hall

Archeology and Paleontology Hall

USEFUL INFORMATION

ADDRESS: Lastra Av and Muñiz St. Ph. 02241 43-0982
HOURS: Summer Season: Tue - Fri: 8 AM to 2 PM, Sat, Sun and Holidays: 9 AM to 1 PM and 5:30 PM to 7:30 PM. Winter Season: Tue - Fri: 9 AM to 3 PM, Sat, Sun and Holidays: 9 AM to 1 PM and 3:30 PM to 5:30 PM.

Pampean Museum Patio decorated with cistern.

Example of gaucho's braid (8 kg - 17,60 lb).

INAUGURATED IN 1941, floors were made of brick, color tiles and slate, the roof was made with girders and it has wide walls.

ARCHEOLOGY AND PALEONTOLOGY HALL

The hall exhibits extinct species in the Pampean soil 8,000 or 10,000 years ago: an interesting glyptodont and the remains of some old humane settlements one thousand seven hundred years old, discovered in 1986.

Glyptodont Carapace.

FIRST PAMPEAN HALL

The hall is devoted to the gaucho's clothes and habits; braided leather crafts and pulperias are exhibited. The hall is in memory of Pedro Nicolás Escribano, founder of San Juan Bautista Guard.

⊕**PLACE.** A large house, replica of the old carrier services with patio and cistern in the middle of the Los Libres del Sur Park. 👁 **WORKS.** More than 11,000 pieces illustrate Chascomús and its inhabitants history from prehistory to the traditional society from 1873 to 1940. ⊙ **IMPOSSIBLE TO MISS.** Pampean halls, daily life objects from 19th and 20th Century, cameras, old photographs and religious imagery. 👄 **OTHERS.** The Museum has a library with 1,500 volumes of regional and local history.

SECOND PAMPEAN HALL

Daily life of the man in the estancia and his relationship with horses is portrayed in outfits, *boleado-ras* (hunting sling), spurs and silver objects such as *mate* pipes belonging to landowners.

DE LOS LIBRES DEL SUR HALL

F. Portela's Red Coat *(punzó)* from 1835.

On November 7, 1839 Los Libres del Sur fought Chascomús battle against the Federal troops. The hall exhibits different badges used by the *Federales* and their red coats named *rojo punzó*. There is also an exhibition of portraits of the conqueror, Prudencio Ortiz de Rosas, an interesting exhibition of coins of that time and a sword, a present from General Lavalle.

CHASCOMUS HALL

The apogee of the traditional society from 1873 to 1940 is depicted with presents from foreign communities, lamps and fans. There is a part in the hall devot-ed to social, cultural and sportive institutions.

Furniture of the era in Chascomús Hall.

MERCEDES J. ALDALUR HALL

Old cameras, a daguerreotype, ambrotype and ferrotype (an example is the oil painting-

photograph of General Mitre) show the connection between Chascomús community and photograph. The hall was named after the museum founder and her memory is preserved here.

RELIGIOUS HALL

Missals, rosaries and imagery are exhibited in the hall. De la Merced Church pulpit, donated in 1900 and several carvings are noteworthy among them a polychrome carving of Santiago Apóstol Matamoros and the Virgen de los Dolores with an embroi-dered black velvet dress.

De la Merced Church Pulpit.

PUBLIC CEREMONY HALL

This small hall is devoted to the Chascomús community activities including seminars, conferences, meetings and temporal exhibitions.

◐ *Going along Lastra until reaching the Costanera, the visitor will turn left to arrive at the Fort.*

FUERTE DE SAN JUAN BAUTISTA | 2

San Juan Bautista Fort. It is a replica of the original fort built in 1979 in celebration of the bicentennial of the city. Surrounded by a palisade with a row of pointed stakes and a large trench, it contains the typical tree lookout, a pulperia and a chapel. Originally San Juan Bautista Fort was located on Independencia Plaza where today is located the Municipality, Casco's House and De la Merced Cathedral.

III COSTANERA AVENUE AND GONZALEZ CHAVEZ STREET. HOURS: EVERY DAY FROM 9 AM TO 12 AM AND 2 PM TO 6 PM.

San Juan Bautista Fort Entrance.

Recreational Area in Chascomús Lagoon.

▶ *Leaving San Juan Bautista Fort, the visitor will return to Costanera España Avenue where Chascomús lagoon is located.*

LAGUNA DE CHASCOMUS | 3

Chascomús Lagoon. The main attraction of the area is the Chascomús lagoon located near the urban area forming part of the system of seven lagoons naturally linked. One of the biggest in Buenos Aires province, the lagoon has 14 km (9 miles) in length and 4 km (2.5 miles) in width, a surface of 3,044 hectares (7,516 acres) and 4 m (13 ft) in maximum depth. A 36 kilometers road surrounds the lagoon where facilities for camping accommodate comfortably tourists. Sports may be practiced around the lagoon. The mentioned road is known as Costanera España when entering Chascomus city. There are institutions devoted to nautical activities and fishing, mainly *pejerrey*.

•▸ MORE INFORMATION ON PAGE 92-93.

THE FIRST FORT

Del Zanjón Fort was created by the first settlers to defend themselves from the Amerindians sudden attacks in 1761 and it was located 26 km (3.1 miles) from Vitel lagoon. Today, there are no traces of it.

▶ *Going along Libres del Sur Street to Route 20 and turning left after crossing Route 2, La Fe Estancia is located 28 kilometers ahead.*

LIBRES DEL SUR

Due to the commercial activity, Libres del Sur is the most important street in Chascomús. De los Italianos Clock, Provincia de Buenos Aires Bank and Telefónica de Argentina building are located on this important street.

ESTANCIA LA FE ⁴

La Fe Ranch. The estancia is located 30 kilometers from the urban area, the Samborombón river runs through the 200 hectares (494 acres) of the estancia lands comprehending a hill of acacias, violets, mint and wild berries. The property contains five comfortable suites with fireplace or furnace operated with firewood. Homemade dishes are served both typical and international. In the estancia facilities, the visitor will be able to practice sports such as volleyball, soccer, bicycle riding, trekking, horse riding and fishing.

III ROUTE 20, 28 KILOMETERS FROM ROUTE 2 CROSSING, KILOMETER 116.5 TOWARDS MAGDALENA. TELEPHONE (02241) 43-6193. EXTENSION 261.

▶ Along Route 20, 38 kilometers ahead towards Ranchos locality, the visitor will turn right to find La Horqueta Estancia.

ESTANCIA LA HORQUETA ⁵

La Horqueta Ranch. Located at the shore of Vitel lagoon five kilometers from the city, the estancia has 200 hectares (494 acres) and a main house in Tudor style erected in 1928; its four

La Fe Estancia Main Entrance.

rooms keep the original furniture from that time. In the house dedicated to guests, there are five rooms more in country style. The swimming pool and the park are visible from the 100 sq m (328 sq ft) meeting room. Old trees of different species, the lagoon and the vast landscape of the plains surround the estancia house. Horse riding, boat riding on the lagoon, *pejerrey* fishing and canoeing are some of the sports the visi-

tor may practice in the facilities.

III ROUTE 20, 4.6 KILOMETERS FROM ROUTE 2 TOWARDS RANCHOS. TELEPHONE: 15-412-0269.

La Horqueta Estancia Guest House.

▶ Returning to Route 20, the visitor will turn right and 11 kilometers ahead turn left to find La Mamaia Estancia.

ESTANCIA LA MAMAIA ⁶

La Mamaia Ranch. This estancia owned by Campomar family is located 200 meters from Route 20 surrounded by poplar and lime trees. The facilities contain a swimming pool and a solarium, a very particular feature in the estancia of the area; the visitor may ride horses, play crocket or ping-pong. The house contains four double rooms; the *asado* is the estancia speciality in Chascomús. ∎

III ROUTE 20, 16 KILOMETERS FROM ROUTE 2 TOWARDS RANCHOS. TELEPHONE (02241) 42-4023.

91

ICHTHYOLOGICAL AWARENESS 👁

In 1947, the Hydrological Station was created to breed pejerrey and to protect the fish very demanded by fishermen in the lagoon.

La Mamaia Estancia Main House.

Río Salado Lagoons

On lands located in the center towards the west of Buenos Aires provinces there are three lacustrine ecosystems Lobos, Monte and Chascomús. The lagoons and their natural environment are ideal for fishing, water sports and watching the interesting fauna in the surroundings.

◀ **AVIS FAUNA.** Among the diversity of birds around Buenos Aires province lagoons, some aquatic birds such as coots are noteworthy *(photo on the left).* Many visitors come to the area to appreciate the birds.

Chajá
◀ (Crested screamer flycatcher.) Usually seen in couples or blocks and characterized by its powerful harsh caw.

Toad
▲ Rarely seen except during floods it belongs to the batrachian group.

Coipu
▲ It is a variety of the nutria, very common in lagoons.

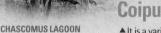

CHASCOMUS LAGOON

SURFACE: Ha 3,000 (7,407 acres)

MONTE LAGOON

SURFACE: Ha 720 (1,777 acres)

CANOEING

The calm waters of these lagoons are ideal for practicing this water sport. For canoeing, one or two rowers use lightweight kayaks or canoes to travel through water. Some institutions in the area provide gear for those interested in keeping in practice this pleasant sport.

Jet Ski

▼ They are motorcycles for water to cross the lagoon with a speed of more than 90 km (56 miles) per hour. Some visitors used them for practicing water-skiing.

Windsurf

▶ During recent years the practice of this sport has become very popular in the area. The traditional Regatas de Chascomús Club founded in 1905 organizes windsurfing courses for all levels.

FISHING. One of the most popular activities in the area due to the great variety of fish found in the lagoons.

▲ *PEJERREY.* Fishermen's favorite.

▲ *TARARIRA.* The most abundant.

▲ **STRIPPED MULLET.** a very tasty fish.

Flamingo

▼ They can be seen in groups and they are distrustful and noticed by their elegant movements and pink color.

LOBOS LAGOON

SURFACE : **Ha** 800 (1,975 acres).

Life in a Diagonal

La Plata is the capital of Buenos Aires province, college students occupy its nice architecture and tree covered diagonal streets imprinting their hectic rhythm. In the suburbs, Pereyra Iraola Park creates a pleasant verdant environment.

CENTRO CULTURAL DARDO ROCHA

LARGE HOUSE IN DEL PARQUE PEREYRA IRAOLA

PARQUE PEREYRA IRAOLA ENTRANCE

CIUDAD DE LOS NIÑOS

LAKE IN PARQUE PEREYRA IRAOLA

MUSEO DE CIENCIAS NATURALES

LA PLATA CATHEDRAL

LEGISLATURA DE LA PLATA

RO ARGENTINO

LA PLATA CATHEDRAL. INTERIOR

OBSERVATORIO ASTRONÓMICO

La Plata and Surroundings

La Plata city, the capital of Buenos Aires province has noteworthy buildings and extensive greenery. Buenos Aires and La Plata are connected by a highway. This itinerary is divided into three sectors. The first one will allow the visitor to discover the monumental aspect of the city; the second one includes the Paseo del Bosque and the Museo de Ciencias Naturales. The third one and last includes a visit to the República de los Niños and Parque Pereyra Iraola.

Sector 1
MONUMENTAL LA PLATA

SIGHTS TO SEE

❶ Cathedral ✱✱✱✱ ❷ Plaza Moreno✱✱
❸ Museo y Archivo Dardo Rocha ✱✱
❹ Municipalidad ✱✱ ❺ Teatro
Argentino ✱✱ ❻ Legislatura ✱✱✱
❼ Plaza San Martín ✱✱ ❽ Pasaje Dardo
Rocha ✱✱✱ ❾ Casa de Gobierno ✱✱

TIME TO ALLOT

In five hours, the sector will be covered, including main buildings and plazas.

Two hour–half will be enough to see the essential parts of the city center.

REFERENCES

E PARKING LOT •〉 PAGE 124 – TRANSPORTATION
i INFORMATION •〉 PAGE 122 – BASIC DATA
🚉 TRAIN STATION •〉 PAGE 124 – TRANSPORTATION
E BUS STATION •〉 PAGE 124 – TRANSPORTATION
✈ AIRPORT •〉 PAGE 124 – TRANSPORTATION

CALLE 46
CALLE 47
CALLE 48
CALLE 49
CALLE 50
AVENIDA 51
AVENIDA 53
CALLE 54
CALLE 55
CALLE 56

CALLE 14
AVENIDA 13
CALLE 12
CALLE 11
CALLE 10
CALLE 9
ACALLE 8
AVENIDA 7
CALLE 6
CALLE 5

DIAGONAL 74
DIAGONAL 80
DIAGONAL 73
DIAGONAL 79

1

BERAZATEGUI

FLORENCIO
VARELA

41

Pereyra
Iraola
Provincial
Park

Va. Elisa

A. del Carnaval

0 km	2.5	5
0 miles	1.5	3

TIME TO ALLOT	Detailed Visit: two days.	
	Rapid Visit: a day.	
DISTANCE	30 km approx. (18 miles).	
MEANS	By car and on foot.	

Sector 2
PASEO DEL BOSQUE

SIGHTS TO SEE

❶ Casa Curutchet ✳✳ ❷ Monumento al Almirante Brown ✳ ❸ Zoológico ✳✳✳
❹ Teatro Martín Fierro ✳✳
❺ Museo de Ciencias Naturales ✳✳✳✳
❻ Observatorio Astronómico ✳✳✳

97

TIME TO ALLOT

⏸ **In five hours,** the Paseo del Bosque will be covered at a relaxed.
▶ **Two and a half hours** will be enough to visit the main points of interest.

TIME TO ALLOT

⏸ **In six hours,** both places may be vivited at a relaxed pace.
▶ **Three hours** will be enough to cover the main points of interest.

Sector 3
LA PLATA SURROUNDINGS

SIGHTS TO SEE

❶ República de los Niños ✳✳✳
❷ Parque Pereyra Iraola ✳✳✳

INSCRIPTIONS

═══ Asphalt Road
╪╪╪ Gravel Road
••••• Graded Earth Road
[123] National Route
[123] Provincial Route

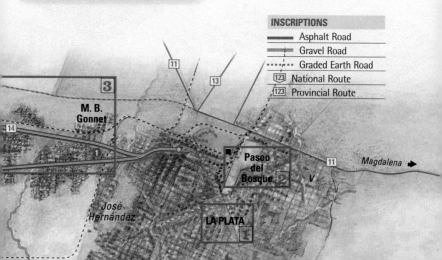

Monumental La Plata

Founded on November 19, 1882 by Dardo Rocha, the city was born to become Buenos Aires province capital. In the urban center, characterized by its diagonal streets, there are monumental buildings such as the Congress, the Cathedral, theaters and museums surrounded by parks.

❺ TEATRO ARGENTINO ✱✱
The cultural complex replaces the old theater destroyed in a fire in 1977.

❸ MUSEO Y ARCHIVO DARDO ROCHA ✱✱
The museum exhibits furniture, works of art, documents and personal objects belonging to Dardo Rocha, the city's founder.

❷ PLAZA MORENO ✱✱
The first stone for the establishment of the city was set in this area in 1882.

❹ MUNICIPALIDAD ✱✱
A tower is set above this magnificent 14,400 sq m (17,225 sq yd) building erected in sober and majestic style.

CALLE 49

AVENIDA 13

CALLE 50

CALLE 14

CALLE 11

CALLE 12 ❹

❸

❷

AVENIDA 51

CALLE 54

AVENIDA 53

CALLE 15

❶

Om 100
Oyd 100

❶ CATHEDRAL ✱✱✱✱
Inaugurated in 1932, the neo Gothic style church has 97 m (318 ft) in height and the construction took half a century.

SIGHTS TO SEE

- **CATHEDRAL**
- **TEATRO ARGENTINO**
- **LEGISLATURA**
- **PASAJE DARDO ROCHA**

FACTS

FOUNDING SPADE
Dardo Rocha Museum and Archive exhibits the spade used to set the first stone in La Plata city on November 19, 1882.

99

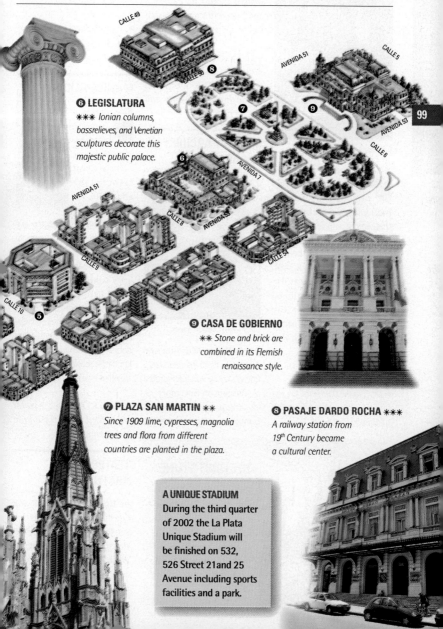

❻ LEGISLATURA
✱✱✱ Ionian columns, bassreliefs, and Venetian sculptures decorate this majestic public palace.

❾ CASA DE GOBIERNO
✱✱ Stone and brick are combined in its Flemish renaissance style.

❼ PLAZA SAN MARTIN ✱✱
Since 1909 lime, cypresses, magnolia trees and flora from different countries are planted in the plaza.

❽ PASAJE DARDO ROCHA ✱✱✱
A railway station from 19th Century became a cultural center.

A UNIQUE STADIUM
During the third quarter of 2002 the La Plata Unique Stadium will be finished on 532, 526 Street 21 and 25 Avenue including sports facilities and a park.

The itinerary starts on 14 Street between 51 and 53 Avenues in La Plata where the Cathedral is erected.

CATHEDRAL 1

Cathedral Main Entrance.

Designed by French architect Pedro Benoit, this neo Gothic style church has five naves in the front part, three in crossing section and a large apsis. The construction started in 1885 and the first stone was laid on April 28, 1884. The building was inaugurated in 1932 and has 5,300 sq m (6,340 sq yd). In the interior, the museum has a list of the names of the people who participated in the construction.

•) MORE INFORMATION ON PAGE 102-103.

▶ Leaving the Cathedral, the visitor will cross 14 Street to arrive at Moreno Plaza.

PLAZA MORENO 2

Moreno Square. The first stone of the plaza set and buried there marks the geometrical center of La Plata. The design was made in such a way that from the central path in the plaza both the Cathedral and the superb Municipal Palace can be appreciated.

▶ On the corner of 12 Street and 50 Street in the plaza, the visitor will cross to 933, 50 Street where Dardo Rocha Museum and Archive has the main entrance.

MUSEO Y ARCHIVO 3 DARDO ROCHA

Dardo Rocha Museum Interior.

Dardo Rocha Museum and Archive. La Plata founder, Dardo Rocha's house was inaugurated as Museum on November 19, 1952, the patrimony exhibited is composed mainly of donations from the founder's descendants composed of furniture, china, cloths and works of art. The main attraction of the museum are those items related to the founding of the city.

III 933, 50 STREET. HOURS: MONDAY THROUGH FRIDAY FROM 9 AM TO 6 PM. TELEPHONE: 15-427-5591.

▶ Along 50 Street the visitor will continue one block to 12 Street to arrive at the Municipality.

MUNICIPALIDAD 4

City Hall. This German renaissance style construction was completed between 1883 and 1886. At the beginning, the building was protected by a fence but in 1910 it was removed and the gardens became part of the city parks. The clock was originally located on the former train station, today Dardo Rocha Walk. The cote of arms of the city, designed by Pedro Benoit is represented on the stained-glass doors of the winter garden.

III 12 STREET, BETWEEN 51 AND 53 STREET. TELEPHONE 15-421-1021.

▶ Along 53 Avenue, the visitor will turn left two blocks to arrive at Argentino Theater.

THE FIRST STONE

On November 19, 1882 the first stone for the construction of the city was laid on Moreno Plaza in the Los Altos de Tolosa. Dardo Rocha supported the project of creating a capital for Buenos Aires Province.

TEATRO ARGENTINO 5

On November 19, 1890, the Argentino Theater raised its curtain for the first time to present the opera *Otello* by Giuseppe Verdi. The theater functioned until 1977 when a fire destroyed part of it. The new building was inaugurated on year 2000 and

The New Argentino Theater.

has a capacity for 2,000 people.
51 STREET, BETWEEN 9 AND 10 STREET.
TELEPHONE 15-429-1742 HOURS: TUES-
DAY THROUGH SATURDAY FROM 10 AM
TO 7 PM. SUNDAY FROM 10 AM TO 5 PM.

▶ *Returning to 51 Avenue, a block ahead on the right side is the Congress.*

LEGISLATURA 6

Sight of the Congress Palace.

Congress. Designed by German engineers Heine and Hagemann, it was inaugurated on May 4, 1883 when the House of Representatives opened; the Senate was inaugurated on May 7, 1889. There are three entrances instead of one identified with porticos containing four columns with Ionian capitals and frontispieces. Italian sculptor Victor de Pol designed the sculptured groups on the portico and the furniture was brought from Paris.

◆▷ MORE INFORMATION ON PAGE 104-105.

▶ *Along 51 Avenue, the visitor will continue to 7 Avenue to find San Martín Plaza.*

PLAZA SAN MARTIN 7

S. Martín Square. A replica of the monument inaugurated in Boulogne Sur Mer in 1909 is located on the center of the plaza to pay honors to the Argentine national hero, San Martín. The superb forestation includes lime, araucaria, cypresses, magnolias and Indian chestnut trees. On one side of the plaza on 54 Street is located one of the most popular spots: the gorgeous iron pavilion brought from France.

▶ *A couple of meters ahead, between 6 Street and 7 Avenue is located Dardo Rocha Walk.*

PASAJE DARDO ROCHA 8

Dardo Rocha Walk. Located on the grounds where Del Sur Railway Station called 19 de Noviembre functioned. Designed by Italian architect Francisco Pinaroli, the sation was moved to the present location on 1 Avenue and 80 Diagonal due to inconvenience of having a train station on the

Entrance Hall of Dardo Rocha Walk.

BRICK OVEN
When La Plata was built, in order to facilitate the construction of the city, 138 brick ovens were set, 3 railroads of 90 km were constructed to transport lime, sand and stones.

middle of the city. In 1926, Governor Monteverde proposed to transform the building of the former station in a complex including offices, shops, a cultural center, halls for concerts, small theaters and a central hall devoted to exhibitions; at the beginning the place was called Monteverde walk, today Dardo Rocha walk.
▦ 50 STREET BETWEEN 6 AND 7 STREET.

▶ *Along 50 Street to 6 Street, the visitor will turn right one block to arrive at the Government House.*

CASA DE GOBIERNO 9

Government House Lateral View.

Government House. The construction of the Government House started in 1883 and lasted nine years. The building contains two symmetrical wings surrounded by interior patios where governmental offices are located. The Governor residence, built in 1911, is located on the same square, on 5 Street. ▪
▦ 60 STREET, BETWEEN 51 AND 53 ST.

101

La Plata Cathedral

The largest neo Gothic style church in the world built in the 20th Century with 106 m (348 ft) length, 66 m (217 ft) in the crossing of the main nave with the lateral one, a surface of 5,300 square meters (57,600 sq foot) and capacity for 14,000 people. The imposing templehas five naves in the front and three in the crossing point. In 1992, the works were resmed and they were finished in 1999.

THE LATERAL TOWERS on the facade correspond to the part of the church finished in 1999 and are 111.7 m (366 ft) in height.

THE FLOOR was set in 1940 was made of granite marble: pink from Olavarria, grey from San Luis and black from Balcarce burnished as a mirror.

THE DOME is supported by four columsn of 9 m (30 ft) in with. The vault containing ribs intersecting its arch, is desingded as a star with eight projecting points (*photo above*).

THE CONFESSION BOOTHS in oak wood, were carved by the same Tirolese artists who made de throne and the seats in the choir.

THE DOORS contain sculptures of the Apostles.

USEFUL INFORMATION

ADDRESS: 14 Street, between 51 and 53.
Telephone: (0221) 427-3504.
HOURS: Mon through Sat from 9 AM to 6 PM and Sun from 9 AM to 1 PM and 3 PM to 8 PM.
GUIDED TOURS: Two different circuits (Church and Museum). Free continually until one hour before closing time.

FACTS

THE SEATS IN THE CHOIR were carved in lime trees. The medallions on the seats present 26 faces of different saints chosen by Moroder.

THE MAIN ALTAR is located on the crossing of the naves for the comfort of the parish (a not very common position in a Gothic church). A subsequent decision in Vatican Council II established this practice.

THE CENTRAL NAVE *is 120 m (393 ft) in length and 36 m (118 ft) in height.*

103

THE ARCHBISHOP *throne carved in lime tree wood with a 8 m (26 ft) in height needle was designed by Tirolese artists M. Schenke and Leo Moroder.*

THE STAINED GLASS art in the rosette and in the lower windows has 262 pieces made of 25,000 enameled glasses.

THE CRYPT on the underground keeps the founder of the city Dardo Rocha and his wife Juana Arana mortal remains, relocated on the place in 1940.

MODELS *of the Statues exhibited in the Museum.*

THE CATHEDRAL MUSEUM has a permanent hall devoted to the men involved in the construction of the church; tools and materials used in the building construction, the style particulars, among other information are presented. It also houses a hall devoted to temporal exhibitions and an auditorium for organizing cultural activities.

Legislatura de La Plata

The Palace where the Buenos Aires Province Legislature functions was designed at the end of 20th Century by German architects Gustavo Heine and Jorge Hagemann in a severe classical style containing elements of German renaissance style. The details in the decoration show the prosperity of the area during the time of the construction.

THE CEILING in the House of Representatives was painted by Argentine artist Graciano Menilharzu.

THE GARDENS
around the building are designed as a plaza decorated with seasonal flowers.

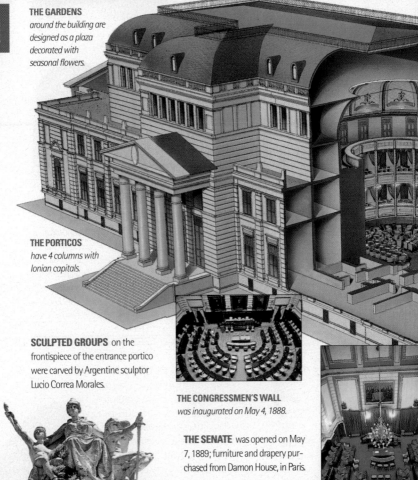

THE PORTICOS
have 4 columns with Ionian capitals.

SCULPTED GROUPS on the frontispiece of the entrance portico were carved by Argentine sculptor Lucio Correa Morales.

THE CONGRESSMEN'S WALL
was inaugurated on May 4, 1888.

THE SENATE was opened on May 7, 1889; furniture and drapery purchased from Damon House, in Paris.

ADDRESS: 7 Street between 51 and 53 Street. Telephone: (0221) 422-8878.

HOURS: Monday through Friday from 8:00 AM to 8 PM.

GUIDED TOURS: Even though there are not organized tours, the Senate Ceremonial Department personnel offer students and tourists special tours.

FACTS

FRIEZES

The three facades have friezes depicting allegorical sculptures made of cement by Italian artist Victor De Pol.

THE CHANDELIER

is located on the middle of the House of Senators hanging 18 m (59 ft) from the ceiling. It was made of bronze with crystal lamps reproducing the form of plants.

THE MAIN STAIRCASE

leading to both Houses has columns with capitals in Corinthian style on both sides.

THE TOWERS

are spherical, made of slate and designed by Floro Durand.

105

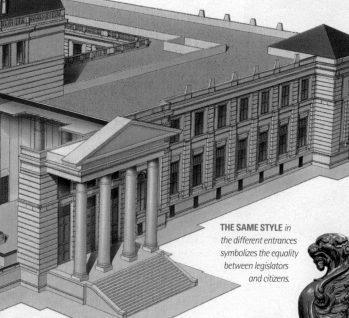

THE SAME STYLE *in the different entrances symbolizes the equality between legislators and citizens.*

THE MAIN ENTRANCES *are three for both Houses. All of them have porticos composed by columns with Ionian capitals crowned by sculptured groups.*

THE PRESIDENTIAL DAIS

in the Senate House has a magnificent carved work accomplished by Parisian wood carvers.

Paseo del Bosque

The most important public park in La Plata city. The park was designed on the place where Pereyra Iraola estancia was located in previous times. It has more than one hundred trees species in 60 hectares (148 acres) area. The emblematic buildings Museo de Ciencias Naturales and Observatorio Astronómico are located there.

❷ MONUMENTO AL ALMIRANTE BROWN ✳

In memory of the Irish sailor who fought for Argentina Independence, the statue and a column are located in the round entrance of the Paseo del Bosque.

NEIGHBORING STADIUMS

Close to the Paseo del Bosque are the soccer stadiums corresponding to La Plata most important teams: Estudiantes and Gimnasia y Esgrima.

AVENIDA 1

AVENIDA 53

AVENIDA IRAOLA

CALLE 2

❹ TEATRO MARTIN FIERRO ✳✳

In summer, the theater functions for ballet performances and popular concerts.

❶ CASA CURUTCHET ✳✳✳

The only project achieved in South America by famous Swiss architect Le Corbusier to function as La Plata physician and surgeon Pedro Curutchet's residence.

SIGHTS TO SEE

- **MUSEO DE CIENCIAS NATURALES**
- **JARDIN ZOOLOGICO**
- **OBSERVATORIO ASTRONOMICO**
- **CASA CURUTCHET**

FACTS

THE CITY OF THE UNIVERSITY
On the city founded by
Dardo Rocha (photograph)
is located an important
university where
70,000 students pursue
their careers annually.

❸ **ZOOLOGICO** ✶✶
Founded in 1907, it is one of the most important zoos in Argentina.

❻ **OBSERVATORIO ASTRONOMICO** ✶✶✶
French scientist and navigator Francisco Beuf designed and accomplished this project on the grounds where the Astronomical and Geophysical School functioned.

107

CAMINO CENTENARIO

ARTIFICIAL LAKE
Inaugurated in 1904 and located opposite Martin Fierro Theater, the grotto leading to the theater was built seven years later.

❺ **MUSEO DE CIENCIAS NATURALES** ✶✶✶✶
Its collections of paleontology and anthropology are renowned worldwide and the museum is one of the best in the country.

The itinerary starts in 53 Avenue opposite República del Líbano small plaza where Curutchet's House and Museum is located.

CASA MUSEO CURUTCHET 1

Curutchet´s House and Museum. In 1948, physician and surgeon Pedro Curutchet commissioned the master of 20th Century mo-dern architecture, Swiss Le Corbusier a project for a residence on 53 Avenue. At the end of 1949 the works started under Argentine architect Amancio Williams supervision. The Swiss architect had suggested the latter to Mr. Curutchet. The mentioned Amancio Williams first, Simón Unger later and finally engineer Alberto Valdés directed the works, finished in 1955. Le Corbusier designed only two houses for the American continent, both for Argentine people but this one was the only one ultimately erected. Since 1989, Buenos Aires Architects Association has functioned in the house.

320, 53 AVENUE. TELEPHONE: 482-2631. TOURS: MONDAY, TUESDAY AND FRIDAY FROM 8 AM TO 2 PM.

Curutchet's House.

▶ Leaving Curutchet's house and going along 53 Avenue until reaching 1 Avenue, the visitor will find Admiral Brown small plaza.

MONUMENTO AL ALTE. BROWN 2

Admiral Brown Monument. The small plaza in memory of Admiral Brown is located opposite Rivadavia Plaza. Brown was an Irish sailor in charge of the Argentine naval forces in the 19th Century. Different governments commis-sioned the sailor to defend the Rio de la Plata

URBAN DESIGN

Engineer Pedro Benoit was in charge of the urban plan for the layout of the city. La Plata has the shape of a perfect square with precise limits encircled by a wide boulevard. The designer included in the project areas of green parks.

entrance from possible invasions. His first assignment aboard *Hércules* Frigate was to conquer Martín García Island and he succeeded on March 15, 1814. This was his first victory for the Argentine Navy and many more followed this one.

▶ Along Iraola Diagonal Avenue one hundred fifty meters ahead, the visitor will find the zoo entrance on the left side.

White Rhinoceros in La Plata Zoo.

ZOOLOGICO 3

Zoo. Engineer Antonio Cravetti designed the park and the museum which opened in 1907 with a collection of birds belonging to Alfredo Plot, the first director of the institution. Today this comprehensive zoo has 71 bird species with more than three hundred specimens, 61 mammal species with 229 specimens and 22 reptile species with 80 specimens. The garden is the natural enviroment for the fauna samples containing more than one thousand different plants belonging to 280 local and exotic species.

IRAOLA AVENUE WITHOUT NUMBER. PHONE (0221) 427-3925. HOURS: TUESDAY THROUGH SUNDAY FROM 9 AM TO 6 PM.

▶ Leaving the Zoo the visitor will continue along Iraola Avenue and will cross the artificial lake to find Martin Fierro Theater.

LA PLATA HIPPODROME 👁
The building housing the racetrack, located opposite the Paseo del Bosque was built by Julio A. Barros in rational style, a very modern style for that time.

Interior of the main floor in La Plata Natural Science Museum.

TEATRO MARTIN FIERRO | 4

Martin Fierro outdoor theater was inaugurated in 1949 and is mainly used during summertime. It is located on the isle on the middle of the artificial lake in Paseo del Bosque. At the entrance República de Francia Plaza shows a Roman style portico. It has a capacity for 2,400 spectators who may enjoy a show surrounded by pergolas and flowerbeds. The Municipality organizes classical music concerts, opera, ballets, popular music concerts, plays for children and different artistic expressions.

▥ PASEO DEL BOSQUE W/N. PHONE: 421-2660. THE CONCERT CALENDARYS AVAILABLE AT DARDO ROCHA WALK.

▶ *Returning to Iraola Avenue, on the left side is located a street leading to the Natural Science Museum.*

MUSEO DE CIENCIAS NATURALES | 5

Natural Science Museum. The Museum was created in 1877 in the Capital Federal with the name Buenos Aires Archeological Museum, later was called Moreno Museum. Seven years later, on July 1884, it was moved to the Buenos Aires province capital as Natural Science Museum; the same year, the construction of the present building started under German architect Heynemman and Swedish architect Aberg supervision. The works ended in 1889 but the Museum opened to the public on November 19, 1888. There are different halls with collections of paleontology, archeology, ethnography, mineralogy, zoology and botany; the

dinosaur skeletons constitute its main attraction. It functions as a research center visited by scientists from all over the world.
↪ MORE INFORMATION ON PAGES 110-113.

▶ *Leaving the Natural Science Museum, the visitor will go along Iraola Avenue towards Camino Centenario to arrive at the Astronomical Observatory.*

OBSERVATORIO ASTRONOMICO | 6

Public Library in the Observatory.

Astronomical Observatory. Founded in 1884, it became part of La Plata University in 1905. Pedro Benoit designed the building in Italian renaissance style with the advice of French astronomer Francisco Beuf, former director of the Naval Observatory in Toulon, France. The instruments were brought from Paris. ∎

▥ PASEO DEL BOSQUE W/NUMBER BETWEEN CAMINO CENTENARIO AND IRAOLA AVENUE. TEL: 483-8810 / 421-7308.

Martin Fierro Theater Facade in the Main Entrance.

Museo de Ciencias Naturales

The Natural Science Museum of La Plata, one of the best of this kind in the world, exhibits, among many pieces, an important collection of fossils (dinosaurs and presents times species) including rare types. It also exhibits an interesting collection of pieces belonging to the Andean and Egyptian cultures.

THE BUILDING, in an elliptical shape 135 m (443 ft) by 70 m (230 ft) with 21 exhibition halls located on two of the four stories. Wandering through the halls, the visitor will be able to have a glimpse at details from the origins of life on earth to the evolution of different cultures.

THE SCIENTIFIC RESEARCH *by professionals and technicians is an important task of the Museum.*

REFERENCES

Geology	Archeology
Paleontology	Botany
Zoology	Exhibitions
Anthropology	Auditorium

INSECTS *displayed in XIII Hall show an incredible diversity.*

STATUES *of smilodon, an extinguished Pampean tiger are located on the stairs at the entrance.*

FRANCISCO P. MORENO (1852-1919). Appointed lifelong director, he donated his personal collections to inaugurate the Museum. During his administration the Museum became prestigious all over the world.

USEFUL INFORMATION

ADDRESS: Paseo del Bosque without number.
Telephone 425-9161 / 9638 / 6134 / 7744.

HOURS: It is open all year round from 10 AM to 6
PM except January 1st, May 1st, December 25

GUIDED TOURS: Guided tours are organized Monday through Friday at 2 PM and 4 PM. Saturday,
Sunday and Holidays at 10:30 AM and 4:30 PM.

FACTS

DARWIN AND THE BULL
At the end of 19th Century,
Charles Darwin requested
a rare kind of bull, *ñato*
to be sent to England;
afterwards he sent it
back to the Museum.

THE HALL DEVOTED TO LATIN AMERICAN ARCHEOLOGY *is noteworthy by the Andean collections and a tracing of the Puerta del Sol.*

THE XVII HALL *devoted to aquatic vertebrates contains a singular South American fish with lungs, a lepidosiren.*

IN THE HALL *devoted to osteology of vertebrates, skeletons of earthly and aquatic animals are found, including the human being.*

ARGENTINE *north-west archeology in hall XXII a collection pottery is exhibited.*

XII HALL *exhibits an octopus.*

THE FRONTISPIECE *in the portico is in neoclassical style, however the building ornamentation contains different elements of American pre-Columbian art.*

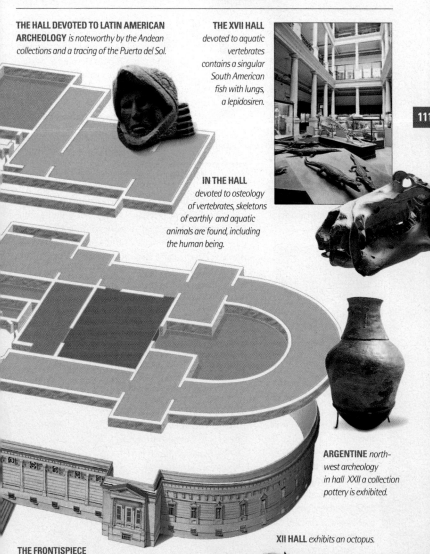

Museo de Ciencias Naturales

Founded in 1877, it is considered one of the five best museums in the world of this kind due to the richness of its collections, the quality of the exhibitions presented and the scientific research pursued there. Visited by more than 600,000 people per year, its halls show to the public data and testimonies of the geological, biological and cultural evolution of earth.

MINERALOGY AND PETROLOGY MAIN FL.

MAIN FLOOR Rock samples and different minerals are exhibited including not only those interesting because of their color and shape but also those important for economic reasons. In the area devoted to the industrial use of minerals, the locations of the country deposits is shown being noteworthy a maquette showing extraction of mineral oil.

A Rhodochrosite, a Type of Marble.

Blue Whale Skull.

ZOOLOGY MAIN FL.

Six halls exhibit the collection including different species belonging to the animal kingdom. There are two halls devoted to invertebrates; one of them exhibits exclusively insects. In the halls devoted to vertebrates the local fauna

is predominant. The species are organized according to the origin of their habitat. The hall devoted to osteology exhibits skeletons of large vertebrates. These halls are mainly visited for those interested in local fauna.

EGYPTIAN HALL MAIN FL.

The hall was inaugurated in 1977 on the occasion of the celebration of the centennial of the museum. The Egyptian collection is considered unique in South America containing Ramses the Second temple found in Aksha (Sudan) recovered when the Aswan dam was built.

PALEONTOLOGY MAIN FL.

Seven consecutive halls display an interesting exposition presenting the different geological periods. The important collections of fossils will allow the visitor to understand better the evolution of plants and animals on earth in different periods. The collection also contains various dinosaur skeletons from all over the world.

Herrerasaurus.

ARGENTINE DINOSAURS

The herrerasuarus from the Valle de la Luna is exhibited together with a titanosaur found in Neuquén and glyptodont carapace among others.

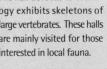

Titanosaur Skeleton.

Assembled Skeleton of an Iguanodon.

Glyptodont Carapace.

⊕ **PLACE.** The exhibition is organized in 21 halls, 16 of them are located on the main floor and 5 on the first floor. ◉ **COLLECTIONS.** Composed of approximately 3,000,000 pieces, some of them exhibited and others kept in laboratories and deposits. ✪ **IMPOSSIBLE TO MISS.** The Egyptian Hall and Latin American Archeology Hall. ◉ **SHOPPING.** The visitor will be able to buy scientific texts and reproductions of remarkable pieces.

Preserved Corpse found in the Chilean Andes, more than 1,300 years old.

113

BIOLOGICAL ANTHROPOLOGY 1st FL.

The exhibition on this hall comprehends ancient humane remains from different times and cultures. Fossils and human beings apparel are organized according to the place of origin. There are also exhibited a preserved corpse buried in a special microclimate and found in the Canary Islands and three complete Egyptian mummies well preserved.

Leather Item Quechua Amerindians.

Perito Moreno Hall Ethnography.

ETHNOGRAPHY 1st FL

Most of the pieces belong to Amerindians groups from Argentina, however there are some belonging to groups from the Arctic, Oceania, Africa and the Amazon region.

Replica of an Inca Crown.

LATIN AMERICAN ARCHEOLOGY 1st FL

Pieces belonging to the important pre-Columbian patrimony are exhibited together with tools corresponding to these cultures comparing them with those used today.

ARGENTINE NORTHWEST ARCHEOLOGY 1st FL

The archeological implements of the Argentina northwest area correspond to the time previous to the Spanish conquest. The items in the collection are divided in four sections according to the different areas of the territory which present distinct ecological characteristics.

Anthropomorphic figure of the Argentine Northwest (NOA).

Pre-Colombian Jar (NOA).

BOTANIC 1st FL

American vegetal life, mainly from Argentina is exhibited in this hall. If the visitor follows the order of the hall, he will be able to appreciate the evolution of botanical plants from ancient times to present times. In this hall, there is an interesting section devoted to nutritional and medicinal usage of some American plants.

La Plata Surroundings

In the northwest area, some kilometers from La Plata, two singular places can be found: La República de los Niños (Children's Republic) a small scale city for the kids recreation, and Parque Pereyra Iraola, a unique green area and forest reserve.

❶ REPUBLICA DE LOS NIÑOS ✳✳✳

Places of interest:

- ● Centro Cívico
- ● Museo del Muñeco
- ● Lago y Aduana
- ● Anfiteatro
- ● Domo

● The kids may ride a boat along the isles, the lake cabanas and the customs *(República de los Niños).*

● Doll Museum Patio *(República de los Niños).*

CITY BELL

GONNET

LARGE SIZE
The original 10,000 ha (24,700 acres) park for public use was reduced to 600 (1,480) after the privatization of the area.

● The Amphitheater *(República de los Niños)* at the shore of the artificial lake where theater performance and seals shows are presented.

✳ SIGHTS TO SEE

- **CENTRO CIVICO**
- **ANFITEATRO**
- **DOMO**
- **PARQUE PEREYRA IRAOLA**

● The Civic Center (*República de los Niños*) is an urban area compiling the most important buildings of this state for kids: small scale palaces, domes, chapels resemble the ambience of a fairy tale.

115

VILLA ELISA

❷ PARQUE PEREYRA IRAOLA ✳✳✳

Located 25 kilometers from La Plata, this 600 hectares (1,500 acres) area is unique in the country containing lakes, forest and a great variety of trees where visitors may ride horses or bicycles.

CHILDREN'S FARM
The *República de los Niños* organizes many educational activities for kids, such as a farm with animals for their instruction.

This section starts in the Children's Republic located in Camino Gral. Belgrano and 501 Street in Gonnet city.

REPUBLICA DE LOS NIÑOS

Children's Republic. Originally, the grounds belonged to the Swift Golf Club, a British food manufacture company settled in the country at the end of 19th Century. Architects Lima, Cueca and Gallo started the construction in 50 hectares (123 acres) area in 1949. On November 26, 1951, President Perón inaugurated the premises with an emotive ceremony. Children visiting this place will be able to play and learn at the same time. The most important institutions are represented in their different buildings so that kids see the basic functioning of a democracy.

III CAMINO GRAL. BELGRANO AND 501 STREET. TELEPHONE: 484-0194. HOURS: MONDAY THROUGH FRIDAY FROM 9 AM TO 6:30 PM, SATURDAY 9 AM TO 11 PM. SUNDAY 9 AM TO 10 PM.

CENTRO CIVICO ①

Pedestrian Area in the Civic Center.

Civic Center. Visited by thousands of kids, the Children's Republic resembles a real city with an urban area containing paths, streets and buildings; this part is known as Civic Center where the most important constructions are found. The buildings corresponding to the government institutions were designed in a similar way to the original ones to attract the kids' fantasy. Other edifices were devised using styles and picturesque expressions of European culture. There is part of the Republic devoted to children stories representing traditional infantile stories such as Andersen narrative, Grimm brothers tales and Tennyson and Mallory legends.

MUSEO DEL MUÑECO ②

Doll House. Inside the Palace of Culture is located the Doll International Museum containing two thousand five hundred pieces depicting dolls with typical attires from fifty countries representing five continents. Probably the house where dolls are displayed is the most visited and favorite in the Children's Republic. There is a historical hall devoted to the classical Tucumán Congress of 1816 with characters and means of transportation from that time; another hall is devoted to Charles Perrault story Cinderella. Artisan Elena Córdoba designed both halls. The last hall is devoted to puppets and marionettes.

Doll Museum Facade.

LAGO Y ADUANA ③

Lake and Customs. Children may ride in a small boat, a replica of those sailing in the Mississippi River. From the boat, children may see the castle, the dome, the amphitheater, the woodcutter hut and the Navy building. The boat sails around the fisherman's isles and his house located on the middle of the lake. The journey ends in the customs building.

Government House located opposite San Martín Plaza in the Children's Republic.

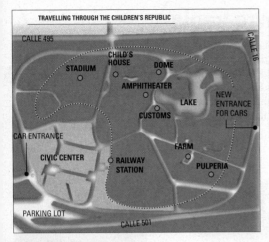

TRAVELLING THROUGH THE CHILDREN'S REPUBLIC

CALLE 495
CALLE 16
STADIUM
CHILD'S HOUSE
DOME
AMPHITHEATER
CUSTOMS
LAKE
NEW ENTRANCE FOR CARS
CAR ENTRANCE
CIVIC CENTER
RAILWAY STATION
FARM
PULPERIA
PARKING LOT
CALLE 501

EDUCATIONAL FARM

The Educational Farm reproduces a stable where children may learn how to milk a cow and how cheese is manufactured. An educational activity dedicated to kids.

▶ *Leaving the Children's city along Camino General Belgrano, the visitor will continue towards Villa Elisa to the Pereyra Iraola entrance on the right side.*

The Lake in Children's Republic.

ANFITEATRO (4)

Amphitheater. This old theater is located opposite the artificial lake. The design was inspired in the ancient Greek theaters where spectators were placed in graded tiers. The stage was also designed following the pattern of the above mentioned theaters. During weekends, children's plays and live music are presented and the theater may be transformed to a lake to present aquatic animals.

DOMO (5)

Dome. La Plata Municipality and the National Commission for Activities related to the Space signed an agreement for the promotion of the country satellite activities among children. The center will have a station for receiving satellite communications and scale models of the Argentine satellites.

The Grand Spacial Dome.

PARQUE PEREYRA IRAOLA |2

117

Pereyra Iraola Park. This immense park is located 25 kilometers from La Plata urban center and is unique in the country due to its large recreational area designed to admit many people. The rest of the parks are usually located in urban areas, therefore the size and purposes are limited. Its 600 hectares (1,480 acres) open to the public offer a verdant area favoring the climate balance in the stretch Buenos Aires and La Plata. Bicycles and horses are available to rent in the park for those who want to tour around and boats or kayaks for sailing on the lakes. ■

○MORE INFORMATION ON PAGE 118-119.

View of the Amphitheater.

Pereyra Iraola Park presents a great variety of trees.

Parque Pereyra Iraola

The Parque Pereyra Iraola constitutes a forest reserve of unique richness with native and exotic species. Located on grounds and buildings of Santa Rosa and San Juan estancias formerly owned by two affluent and traditional families.

SANTA ELENA CHAPEL is near the main building of the old Santa Rosa estancia. The chapel has offered religious services since old times.

THE INTERIOR OF THE CHAPEL *has an altar decorated with magnificent murals.*

THE MAIN BUILDING corresponding to Santa Rosa estancia was finished in 1918, and today houses the park administration.

THE OMBU is a native plant growing together with plane and pine trees.

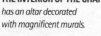

THE PARK was designed by Belgian Carlos Vereecke. Some people believe that Prilidiano Pueyrredón participated in the works.

USEFUL INFORMATION

LOCATION: There are four entrances to the park on Camino Centenario (Provincial Route 14) and General Belgrano (Provincial Route 1) , located on the crossing of both routes. Telephone (0221) 487-0221.

ACTIVITIES: During summertime, bicycles, horses and boats may be rented every day and during the rest of the year on weekends and holiday.

FACTS

THE FIRST EUCALYPTUS In San Juan Estancia park the first eucalyptus seeds received by Domingo F. Sarmiento from Australia were planted.

THE PARK offers visitors 600 hectares (1,480 acres) of greenery located around the main house in Santa Rosa Estancia, former Iraola family estate.

119

ON JUAN MARÍA GUTIERREZ *roundabout is the entrance arch to Pereyra Iraola Park. The interior path travels from the entrance to the recreational area.*

IN 1949 when the estancias were expropriated, there were 132 trees species with more than 20 varieties of eucalyptus and other exotic types.

CATAMARAN ON THE DELTA

RESTAURANT MARIA, LUJAN

SHOPPING CENTER AND TREN DE LA COSTA

LINEA MITRE, BUENOS AIRES TRAINS

SALA DE ESP

RURAL HANDICRAFTS

RESTAURANT LA ROSA NEGRA

SPA AQUA SULIS, LOBOS

HANDMADE PENCILS AT TIGRE

SERVICES

Useful Data

This section contains all the information necessary to help visitors enjoy these itineraries to the maximum. It includes data on transport and the routes to the places of greatest interest, as well as a select list of restaurants serving the finest food, hotels, tourist spots, telephone numbers and other useful tips. It also has suggestions on where to buy traditional products.

PUERTO DE FRUTOS IN TIGRE

RIVER FERRY ON THE LUJAN RIVER

TAXIS EN AV. R. S. PEÑA Y FLORIDA

SUMMARY

TIGRE TRAIN STATION

HOTEL LAURA

RESTAURANT LA CABALLERIZA

LA CABALLERIZA

BOLETERIA Y TELEGRAFO

JEFE

CHASCOMUS TRAIN STATION

Practical Information

The areas around the city of Buenos Aires have an excellent service infrastructure for tourists. All the towns have banks, currency exchange offices, post offices, national and international telephone exchanges and emergency services.

MEDICAL AND EMERGENCY SERVICES

The public hospitals in the areas around the city of Buenos Aires provide free medical assistance, 24 hours a day, 365 days a year. Inthe event of a medical emergency, ring SAME (Servicio de Atención Médica de Emergencia) on107 (toll-free, using any telephone) or 4923-1050.

A SAME ambulance.

TOURIST INFORMATION

▌ **Dirección de Turismo de Escobar** Mitre 787. Tel. (03488) 43-0550/0546.
▌ **Dirección de Turismo de Luján** San Martín 550. Tel. (02323) 42-0453.
▌ **Dirección de Turismo de San Miguel del Monte** Costanera Av. and Fray Martinez. Tel. (02271) 42-1138.
▌ **Dirección de Turismo de Tigre** Mitre and Italia Av. Tel. 4512-4497/98.

▌ **Dirección de Turismo de San Antonio de Areco** Zerboni and Avellano. Tel. (02326) 45-3165.
▌ **Dirección de Turismo de La Plata** Calle 50, corner 6. Tel. (0221) 427-1535.
▌ **Departamento de Turismo de Lobos** Salgado 40. Tel. (02227) 43-1450/1455.

TELEPHONE AREA CODES

▌ **Chascomús:** 02241.
▌ **Pilar:** 02322.
▌ **Luján:** 02323.
▌ **S. A. de Areco:** 02326.
▌ **Lobos:** 02227.
▌ **S. M. del Monte:** 02271.
▌ **La Plata:** 0221.

SERVICES SCHEDULE

As in other parts of the country, many stores and services in towns in Buenos Aires province close between noon and 4 PM; however, in more densely populated areas they do not close for lunch.
▌ **Bank schedule**
Mon-Fri, from 10 AM to 3 PM.
▌ **Currency exchange office schedule**
Mon-Fri, from 10 AM to 5 PM.
▌ **Store schedule**
Monday-Friday, from 9 AM to 7 PM; Saturdays, from 9 AM to 1 PM. Shopping centers and shopping areas are open longer.

CREDIT CARDS

Visitors can make purchases using all the main credit cards. Some establishments may ask to see some ID.

LOSS OR THEFT OF CREDIT CARDS

▌ **American Express**
4310-3165 y 4312-1661.
▌ **Cabal**
0800 555-2222.
▌ **Diners**
0810 444-2484.
▌ **Mastercard** (issued in Argentina) 4340-5700.
▌ **Mastercard** (issued in other countries) 0800 555-0507.
▌ **Visa**
4379-3333.

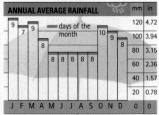

ANNUAL AVERAGE RAINFALL		mm	in
days of the month		120	4.72
9 7 9	10	100	3.94
8	9 8	80	3.15
8 8 8 8 8		60	2.36
		40	1.57
		20	0.78
J F M A M J J A S O N D		0	0

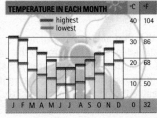

TEMPERATURE IN EACH MONTH	°C	°F
highest lowest	40	104
	30	86
	20	68
	10	50
J F M A M J J A S O N D	0	32

CLIMATE

Average temperatures in winter are 12°C (54°F) and in summer 24°C (75°F). Annual average rainfall is 1,000 mm (394 in).

LOCAL HOLIDAYS

9 JULIO Independencia

Many towns and villages hold local festivals during which their day-to-day charm becomes particularly spectacular. For example, November 10 is the Día de la Tradición in San Antonio de Areco, a day when they hold races and other activities involving traditional skills. There is also the Día de la Virgen, held in Luján on December 8, while in Escobar the third week of September is devoted to La Fiesta Nacional de la Flor, a traditional flower festival which is held on a speciallydesigned site.

MAIL

Visitors can send letters, postcards and telegrams or buy stamps at the Correo Argentino offices.

█ Chascomús
211 Dorrego.

█ Escobar
302 Rivadavia.

█ La Plata
4 and 51 streets.

█ Lobos
Chacabuco and Cardoner.

█ Luján
571 Mitre.

█ Tigre
1140 Cazón Av.

Airmail letters from different parts of the world.

█ San Antonio de Areco
Aristóbulo del Valle and Alvear.

█ Pilar
451 Pedro Lagrave.

ON-LINE INFORMATION

There are a number of websites with information on the Buenos Aires area:
www.sectur.gov.ar
www.tigretienetodo.com.ar
www.laplata-online.com.ar
www.laplatavive.com.
www.arecoturismo.com.ar
geocities.com/islamartingarcia

USEFUL PHONE NUMBERS

These numbers are toll-free using any telephone:

█ National operator: 19.
█ International operator: 000.
█ Collect calls to other countries: 0800 222-7222.
█ Fire service: 100.
█ Police: 101.
█ Civil defense: 103.
█ Environmental emergencies: 105.
█ Shipping emergencies: 106.
█ Medical emergencies: 107.

█ Information: 110.
█ Time 113.
█ Calls from persons with normal hearing to persons using hearing aids or with speech difficulties: 125.
█ Calls from persons using hearing aids or with speech difficulties to persons with normal hearing: 126.

Mariana López
Austria 123
C 1242 ACF - Buenos Aires
ARGENTINA

0800 555-0016

State Tourism Department information center

This number has information on tourism in the areas around the city of Buenos Aires.

How to Travel

There are lots of different types of transport that visitors can use for traveling around the area: buses, trains, boats, hire cars and a large network of roads and highways which connect the main points of interest to the city. Visitors can also travel around the region by airplane.

TRIPS OUT OF BUENOS AIRES

Buenos Aires has modern highways which cross the city to the suburbs located west, north and south of the city. Four of the five main highways connect up with main roads which run from Buenos Aires out to the Argentine interior. The La Plata-Buenos Aires highway begins at Puerto Madero.

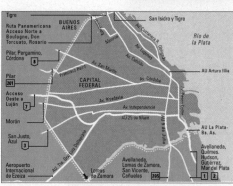

CAR RENTAL

- **Avis** R. Panamericana, km 50, Pilar. Tel. (02322) 47-3505.
- **Rent a Car** RN 8 and Alsina, Pilar. Tel. 0800 6666-247.
- **Excellence** 100 Rolón, local 14, San Isidro. Tel. 4723-4200.
- **Rent a Car** 13 Av. and 32, La Plata. Tel. (0221) 483-5851.
- **Autolisto** 828 122 Av., La Plata. Tel. (0221) 427-6800.

DRIVERS LICENSES

In order to validate a foreign drivers license, call the Automóvil Club Argentino (4802-0522). Chilean and Uruguayan drivers licenses are valid if drivers enter the country using their own automobile.

ROAD TOLLS

Drivers are charged tolls on highways and on some roads through Buenos Aires. The toll varies according to distance traveled, and must be paid at the toll booths (*photo*). Drivers may pay in cash, and there are fast lanes for drivers with the correct change. Credit cards may also be used, though in this case the driver must buy a magnetic chip which is mounted on the windshield, and then drive through the toll booths using the lanes specially allocated for this system.

TRAVELING BY TRAIN

Several of the areas and towns around Buenos Aires can be reached by train. Trains leave from Retiro for Pilar and Tigre, while trains for La Plata, Cañuelas and Chascomús leave from the station at Plaza Constitución. Trains to Luján leave from the Plaza Once railway terminal.

4310-0700

Terminal de Omnibus de Retiro

Use this number to contact bus companies at Retiro Bus Terminal and to check their destinations, schedules, bus frequency and fares to the areas around Buenos Aires.

LONG-DISTANCE BUSES

Buses leave from Retiro bus terminal to all parts of Argentina, as well as to some cities in neighboring countries. Passenger comfort and fares vary from company to company. There are also express bus services which make fewer stops and include bunks for sleeping.

BREAKDOWN SERVICES

For mechanical assistance or a tow truck service on the highways and some main roads, call using a cellphone or the emergency telephones provided. Argentina does not have a state – run breakdown service – the most comprehensive private assistance network is that of the Automóvil Club Argentino, though you must be a member.

125

S.O.S.

Traffic signs.

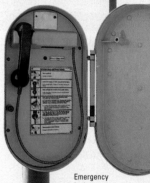

Emergency telephone on the highways

HISTORICAL TRAIN
FACTS

The Tren de la Costa leaves the Retiro terminal for Tigre. The line runs alongside the river and stops off at some old stations that have been restored.

RIVER TRANSPORT

A number of boats sail from Buenos Aires for Colonia, Montevideo and Punta del Este, in Uruguay. The main ferry companies are:

▌ **Buquebús.** Tel. 4316- 6500.
▌ **Fast Ferry.** Tel. 4362-0110.
▌ **Ferry Líneas.** Tel. 4314-2300.

BOATS AND CATAMARANS

In Tigre there are several catamaran and ferryboat lines which travel along the main rivers in the Delta. Visitors can also go on catamaran trips, which range from a one-hour trip to a full day, to visit Isla Martín García or even Uruguay.

• **Interisleña** 4731-0261 / 63.
• **Sturla** 4731-1300.
• **Cacciola** 4749-0329 / 0931.
• **Delta Argentino** 4731-1236.

OTHER TRANSPORS

Visitors can also take a plane from the Aeropuerto de San Fernando and fly over the islands of the delta and Isla Martín García. For more information, call 15 4936-1442. Or you can also use alternative transport to travel around the delta. Call 4728-2865 and 15 5110-1681.

Where to Sleep

There is a wide range of accommodation available in the towns around Buenos Aires, ranging from hostels, inns and campsites all the way up to five star hotels which offer the finest and most luxurious possible services.

ITINERARY 1

HOTELS

Aeronavegantes
Río Carapachay, Tigre.
Tel. 4728-0033. 📞📺☰✕🍸
Park and games courts.
Function room for 150 persons.

Alpenhaus
Arroyo Rama Negra, Tigre.
Tel. 4728-0422.
📞📺✳☰✕🍸
2,500 meters of park area.
Private mooring. Bungalows.
Traditional German beer
house and teahouse.

Atelier Hostería
Río Capitán, Tigre.
Tel. 4731-3532.
📞✳☰✕🍸
With private mooring and
heliport. Bungalows. More
information on page 38.

Bora Bora Hostería
392 Río Sarmiento, Tigre.
Tel. 4728-0646.
📞📺✳☰✕🍸

Bosque de Bohemia
410 Arroyo Antequera, Tigre.
Tel. para reservas 4728-0053.
📞📺✳☰✕🍸
Only one hour from Tigre.

Hostal Delta
Río Luján and Abra Vieja, Tigre.
Tel. 4717-4648 y 4728-0396.
🛎☁✳✕🍸⚓
Fifteen minutes from Tigre.
You will need your own
transport to get here.

Hostería Martín García
Isla Martín García.
Tel. para reservas 4749-0329 /
0931 / 2369 y 4728-0119.
📞📺✳☰✕🍸
The only accommodation
on the island.

I'Marangatú Hostería
Río San Antonio, Tigre.
Tel. 4728-0203/0752.
📞📺✳☰✕🍸
Hires out jet skis for use
on the river.

Laura Hotel & Resort ★★★
Río Paraná de las Palmas, Tigre.
Tel. 4728-1019/2760.
📞📺✳☰✕🍸⚓
Private mooring for boats
and open-air sports areas.

ON-LINE INFORMATION
The official website of the
State Tourism Department
(www.turismo.gov.ar)
contains lists of hotels,
accommodation and rural
tourism establishments
in Buenos Aires.

Centro Náutico Delta
*Río Luján and Canal
Benavídez, Tigre.*
Tel. 4728-0407 / 0410.
☁✳✕🍸⚓
Owned by the Automóvil Club
Argentino (ACA). Get there
by land on Ruta 27 or by water
in a Delta Argentino boat.

Colonia Banco Provincia
34 Río Capitán, Tigre
Tel. 4728-0524 / 0392 / 0426
🛎📺☰✕🍸⚓

Don Gobbi Hostería
*Arroyo Pajarito and
Canal de Vinculación,
San Fernando.*
Tel. 4728-0437 / 4701-9853.
☰✕🍸

El Fondeadero
Canal Honda, Tigre.
Tel. 4749-5379 y 4728-0428.
🛎☁✳☰✕🍸

El Tropezón
*Río Paraná de las Palmas
and Canal de la Serna, Tigre.*
Tel. 4728-1012.
🛎☰✕🍸

Bed & Breakfast
557 Lavalle, Tigre.
Tel. 4749-2499.
🛎☰✕

REFERENCES

✥	STAR CATEGORY	♈	BAR
🛏	DOUBLE ROOM	🏊	SWIMMING POOL
☎	TELEPHONE	▣	LAUNDRY
📺	TELEVISION	🅴	CAR PARK
❄	AIR-CONDITIONING	🛆	TENTS
≋	CENTRAL HEATING	🍹	HOT WATER
✕	RESTAURANT	♨	FIREPLACE

◼ Boraso
Arroyo Boraso, Tigre.
Tel. 4745-2594.
≋ ✕ ♈

◼ Las Rosas
Río Sarmiento, Tigre.
Tel. 4728-2757.
🏊 🍹 ✕ ♈

ITINERARY 2

▤HOTELS▤

◼ Sheraton Pilar ★★★★★
Ruta Panamericana Km 49.3,
Pilar. Tel. (02322) 47-4400.
☎ 📺 ❄ ≋ ✕ ▣ 🅴 🏊 ♈
This hotel has two marvelous restaurants: Don Giovanni and Las Vasijas.

◼ Resort de Campo y Polo
★★★★★
Ruta 6 and Río Luján, Open.
Door. Tel. (02323) 49-6669.
☎ 📺 ❄ ≋ ✕ ▣ 🅴 🏊 ♈
This luxurious resort lies only ten minutes from the city of Luján. As well as the football pitches and tennis courts, it has a heated swimming pool, a golf course and a private heliport.

◼ Catedral ★★★
1074 9 de Julio, Luján.
Tel. (02323) 43-0670.
☎ 📺 ❄ ≋ 🅴 ♈

◼ Biarritz ★★★
Lezica and Torrezuri, Luján.
Tel. (02323) 42-1230.
☎ 📺 ❄ ≋ 🅴 ♈

◼ Del Virrey ★★
129 San Martín, Luján.
Tel. (02323) 42-1658.
☎ 📺 ≋ 🅴 ♈

◼ Hoxon ★★★★
1760 9 de Julio, Luján.
Tel. (02323) 42-9970.
☎ 📺 ❄ ≋ 🅴 ✕ ♈ 🏊

◼ De la Paz ★★
1054 9 de Julio, Luján.
Tel. (02323) 43-4419/42-8742.
☎ 📺 ≋ ✕ ♈

◼ Los Monjes ★★★
981 Francia, Luján.
Tel. (02323) 42-0606.
☎ 📺 ❄ ≋ 🅴

◼ Hotel Fuaz ★★★
448 Dr. Smith Av.,
San Antonio de Areco.
Tel. (02326) 45-2487.
☎ 📺 ❄ ≋ 🅴 ✕ ♈

◼ Hostería del Palomar
Camino Guiraldes and Arellano,
San Antonio de Areco.
Tel. (02326) 45-2012.
☎ ≋ ✕ ♈

◼ La Posada del Ceibo ★★★
Irigoyen between Ruta
Nacional N° 8 and Dr. Smith
Av., San Antonio de Areco.
Tel. (02326) 45-4614 / 45-3128.
☎ 📺 ≋ ✕ 🏊 ♈

◼ Posada Café de las Artes
70 Bolívar, San
Antonio de Areco.
Tel. (02362) 1551-1684.
☎ ❄ ≋ ✕ ♈

◼ Residencial El Hornero
250 Moreno,
San Antonio de Areco.
Tel. (02326) 45-2733.
☎ 📺 ≋ ✕

◼ Residencial San Cayetano
Don Segundo Sombra and
Rivadavia, San Antonio de Areco.
Tel. (02326) 45-2166 / 45-6393.
☎ 📺 ≋ ✕

◼ Estancia La Aurora
8 km. from junction on ruta 41
and ruta 8, San Antonio de
Areco. Tel. (02326) 45-4515 /
45-4219. ☎ ≋ ✕

◼ Los Abuelos
Zerboni and Zapiola,
San Antonio de Areco.
Tel. (02326) 45-6390.
☎ 📺 ≋

San Carlos
Zerboni and Zapiola, San Antonio de Areco. Tel. (02326) 45-3106.
📞 📺 ⅲ ✕ Ⓔ 🏊

Victoria
136 Lavalle, Luján.
Tel. (02323) 42-0582.
📞 📺 ⅲ

Royal
696 9 de Julio, Luján.
Tel. (02323) 42-1295.
📞 📺 ⅲ
18 rooms, and only a few blocks from the downtown.

Centro Hotel
1062 Francia, Luján.
Tel. (02323) 42-0667.
📞 📺 ⅲ Ⓔ
17 rooms.

Brown
2 Almirante Brown, Luján.
Tel. (02323) 42-0623.
📞 📺 ⅲ

Carena
114 Lavalle, Luján.
Tel. (02323) 42-9884.

CAMPSITE

La Porteña
Entrance on RP 41, San Antonio de Areco. Tel. (02326) 45-3402. Auto-camping.

River Plate
Aristóbulo del Valle and Alvear, San Antonio de Areco.
Tel. (02326) 45-1017/2744.

El Triángulo
RN 7, km 69.5, Luján.
Tel. (02323) 43-0116.

Huellas
de la Naturaleza
Camino Carlos Keen, Luján.
Tel. (02323) 43-4972.

ITINERARY 3

HOTELS

Hostería Laguna del Monte ★★★
Costanera Av. and Sardén, San Miguel del Monte.
Tel. (02271) 42-0687 📞 ⅲ 🍸

Country Club ★★
RP 41, km 172, Lobos.
Tel. (02227) 43-0180.
📞 📺 ⅲ Ⓔ ✕
35 rooms and first-class services available.

Bosnia ★
Lamadrid Av. and Córdoba, Chascomús. Tel. (02241) 42-3337.
📞 📺 ⅲ ✕

Laguna ★
Libres del Sur and Maipú, Chascomús. Tel. (02241) 43-6236. 📞 📺 ❋ ⅲ Ⓔ 🍸

Hostería Las Cabañas
Costanera Av. and El Zorzal San Miguel del Monte.
Tel. (02271) 42-0951.
📞 📺 ⅲ

Aqua Sulis Spa Resort
250 Independencia, Lobos.
Tel. (02227) 42-4330 / 1931.
📞 📺 ⅲ ✕ 🔲 🏊

El Jardín
367 Petracchi, S. Miguel del Monte. Tel. (02271) 42-0019.
📞 📺 ⅲ Ⓔ

El Mirador
485 Belgrano, Chascomús.
Tel. (02241) 1567-6438.
📞 ⅲ

El Pescador
Ruta 205, km 110, Lobos.
Tel. (02227) 49-4114.
📞 ⅲ 🍸

Chascomús Hotel
367 Lastra Av., Chascomús.
Tel. (02241) 42-2968.
📞 📺 ⅲ

Libertad
Libertad Av. and RP 205, Cañuelas.
Tel. (02226) 42-2609.
📞 📺 ⅲ

Costanera
Costanera Av. and Castelli, Chascomús. Tel. (02241) 42-2080.
📞 📺 ⅲ
30 rooms, open all year.

Central Park
77 Junín, Lobos.
Tel. (02227) 43-0165.
📞 📺 ⅲ 🏊 🍸

ESTANCIA LA MARTINA

This ranch, which specializes in the sport of polo, offers first-class accommodation, with 16 suite rooms and a club-house. Situated in the town of Vicente Casares.

Los Vascos
Castelli and Costanera Av.,
Chascomús. Tel. (02241).
42-2856 ☎ 📺 ⅲ **E**

Apart Casablanca
Tucumán and Orzali,
Chascomús. Tel. (02241)
43-6420. ☎ 📺 ⅲ **E**

Class Hotel
Belgrano and Almafuerte,
Lobos. Tel. (02227) 43-0090.
☎ 📺 ⅲ

La Antigua Casona
419 Santos Molina, San Miguel
del Monte.Tel. (02271) 42-0512.
☎ 📺 ⅲ **E** 🍸

9 de Julio
241 9 de Julio, Lobos.
Tel. (02227) 42-1465.
☎ 📺 ⅲ

Cañuelas Hotel
Rivadavia and Basavilbaso,
Cañuelas. Tel. (02226) 42-2724.
☎ 📺 ⅲ

Nuevo Colón
70 Libres del Sur, Chascomús.
Tel. (02241) 42-3846.
☎ 📺 ⅲ **E**

≡ CAMPSITE ≡

Bahía de los Lobos
Ruta 205, km 111, Lobos.
Tel. (02227) 49-4294.
It has showers, a store
and a cooking area.

Monte Brown
Camino de circunvalación
s/n, Chascomús.
Tel. (02241) 42-5522.

Club de Pesca
Costanera Av. and Eva Perón,
San Miguel del Monte.
Tel. (02271) 42-0506.

ITINERARY 4

≡ HOTELS ≡

Acuarius ★★★
731 3 Street, La Plata.
Tel. (0221) 421-4229.
☎ 📺 ⅲ ✕ 🖥 **E** 🍸

Argentino ★★★
536 46 Street, La Plata.
Tel. (0221) 423-4111.
☎ 📺 ⅲ 🖥 **E** 🍸
This hotel has a large conference room and offers room
service, valet parking, laundry
and private security guards.

Benevento ★★★
645 2 Street, La Plata. Tel. (0221)
489-1078. 📺 ✕ ⅲ 🖥 **E** 🍸

Catedral ★★★
965 49 Street, La Plata.
Tel. (0221) 423-2020.
☎ 📺 ✕ ⅲ 🖥 **E** 🍸

Corregidor ★★★★
1026 6 Street, La Plata.
Tel. (0221) 425-6800.
☎ 📺 ✕ ⅲ ✕ 🖥 **E** 🍸
The only four-star hotel in La
Plata. It features the La Giralda
snack bar among its amenities.
All-day trips to places of interest

CARLOS THAYS
The French architect
and landscape gardener
Carlos Thays designed
many different gardens
and avenues on
Argentinian ranches —
for example, the one
around the old La
Candelaria ranch —
house in Lobos.

---

are organized from the hotel.
The rooms are very tastefully
decorated.

Del Rey ★★★
180 Plaza Paso, La Plata.
Tel. (0221) 425-1604.
☎ 📺 ✕ ⅲ **E**

El Diamante ★★
565 41 Street, La Plata.
Tel. (0221) 482-7912.
☎ 📺 ✕ ⅲ 🖥 **E** 🍸

La Plata ★★★
783 51 Street, La Plata.
Tel. (0221) 422-9090.
☎ 📺 ✕ ⅲ 🖥 **E** 🍸
Outstanding service.

Roga ★★
Calle 54 N° 384 , La Plata.
Tel. (0221) 421-9553.
☎ 📺 ✕ ⅲ 🍸

≡ ESTANCIAS ≡

El Destino
Located 120 km (70 mi) from
Buenos Aires and 18 km
(11 mi) south of the city
of Magdalena, on the banks
of the Río de La Plata.
Tel. number in Buenos Aires:
4803-6290. ☎ ⅲ ✕ 🖥 **E** ♨
This ranch, which is over
1,850 hectares (4,625 acres)
in size, belongs to the Fundación Elsa Shaw de Pearson.

Juan Gerónimo
Situated in Verónica, 165 km
from Buenos Aires.
Tel. (02221) 48-1414
Tel. (Buenos Aires): 15 4937-
4326 y 4804-9777
☎ 📺 ⅲ ✕ 🖥 **E** ♨
The Tudor-style ranch house
stands in an attractive
natural coastal setting.

Rural Tourism

Most of the estancias open to the public are located in the surrounding areas of San Antonio de Areco, Capilla del Señor and the linked lagoons. The visitor will be able to enjoy a peaceful country environment and typical dishes plus engaging in rural activities such as horse riding, walks and different sports.

ESTANCIAS

Most of the estancias open to tourists and establishments for rural tourism are located on the area comprehending Itinerary 2 of this guide.

INSCRIPTIONS

▬▬▬	Asphalt Road
═══	Gravel Road
••••••	Graded Earth Road
123	National Route
123	Provincial Route

ENTRE RIOS — URUGUAY
BUENOS AIRES
Enlarged Area
Río de la Plata
BUENOS AIRES

Duggan • — San Antonio de Areco — Capilla del Señor — Escobar
Carmen de Areco — Azcuénaga — Los Cardales — Matheu
San Andres de Giles — Torres • — Open Door — Pilar
Gouin • — Carlos Keen • — Luján
Rivas • — Jáuregui • — Olivera • — General Rodríguez — Moreno
Mercedes

❶ La Bamba

Provincial Route 31, located 14 km (11 mi) from San Antonio de Areco. Phone (02326) 45-6293. In Buenos Aires: Phone 4743-314. 🏠☎✕⚓▲⛵
This historical establishment devoted to agricultural and cattle raising activities keeps the buildings from the 19th Century and has a park of 16 hectares.

•) More information on page 65.

❷ El Ombú

Provincial Route 31, 1 km (19 mi) from San Antonio de Areco. Phone (02326) 49-2080. In Buenos Aires: Phone 4821-1876/1130. 🏠☎✕⚓▲⛵
Built in 1880. Horses or sulkies, countryside chores, tennis, golf.

•) More information on page 64.

La Bamba

REFERENCES

🛏 DOUBLE ROOM
☎ TELEPHONE
✕ RESTAURANT
🏊 SWIMMING POOL
🐴 HORSE RIDING
🍖 TYPICAL DISHES
🏃 SPORTS

Old Aimbu

❸ El Rosario de Areco
RP 41 (asphalt), San Antonio de Areco. Tel. (02326) 45-1008.
🛏☎✕🏊🐴🏃🍖
The main house was built in 1892 in colonial criollo style and the park has 12 ha (30 acres) The visitor may stay overnight, enjoy typical and homemade dishes and the famous asado criollo.

❹ Los Patricios
Provincial Route 41, 4 km (25 mi) from San Antonio de Areco. Phone (02326) 45-3823.
🛏☎✕🏊🐴🏃🍖
The visitor may ride horses, stroll around the spacious park and practice sports such as polo, horse riding, swimming and paddle.

❺ Santa María de Todos los Angeles
Provincial Route 192, located 5 km (3 mi) from Open Door. Phone (011) 4802-5449.
🛏☎✕🏊🐴🏃🍖
A green and peaceful oasis where polo and golf may be practiced.

❻ Haras Ternura Ranch
Route 192 Kilometer 8.5, Open Door. Phone (02323) 49-6093.
🛏☎✕🏊🐴🏃🍖
Remodelled stud, spa, swimming pool, gym, restaurant.

❼ Los Viejos Ombúes
Provincial Route 193, Capilla del Señor. Phone (02323) 49-2336.
🛏☎✕🏊🐴🏃🍖
To stroll around the tree-covered park may be rewarding.

❽ La Posesiva
Provincial Route 193, located 14 km (8 mi) from Capilla del Señor. Phone (02326) 49-2252.
🛏☎✕🏊🐴🏃🍖
Spacious park, swimming pool and barbecue.

❾ La Encantada
Provincial Route 193, Capilla del Señor. Phone (02323) 49-2063
🛏☎✕🏊🐴🏃🍖
Cozy country lodging where the tourist may choose between riding horses or flying a balloon above the area.

❿ Los Talas
Route 47, km 23, Luján. Phone (02323) 49-4995.
🛏☎✕🏊🐴🏃🍖
Built in 1824, the main house keeps furniture, chinaware, a wardrobe from that time. The facilities offer horse riding, photographic safaris and bird watching.

⓫ San Ceferino
Provincial Route 6, Open Door. Phone. (02323) 44-1500.
🛏☎✕🏊🐴🏃🍖
A colonial style main house offers a collection of mates and countryside memorabilia. The visitor may take part in the rural chores.

A DAY'S JOURNEY

Some estancias do not offer lodging, however the visitor can spend a day in the country participating in rural chores.

⓬ La Cinacina
Bartolomé Mitre St, San Antonio de Areco. Phone. (02326) 45-2773.
•❯ More information on page 64.

⓭ Resort de Campo y Polo
Provincial Route 6 and Río Luján, Open Door. Phone.(02323)49-6669.

131

ESTANCIAS

The area called linked lagoons corresponding to Itinerary 3 concentrates many important estancias, some of them connected to historical events such as Santa Rita, La Candelaria and La Concepción.

INSCRIPTIONS

▬▬▬	Asphalt Road
═══	Gravel Road
•••••••	Graded Earth Road
123	National Route
123	Provincial Route

❷ Santa Rita
Located 2 km (1.2 mi) from Antonio Carboni, Lobos. Phone. (02227) 49-5026.

One of the oldest estancias in the area, the visitor may practice sports and participate in rural chores.
•) More information on page 78.

❸ San Agustín
Provincial Route 205, located 20 km (12 mi) from Lobos. Phone. (011) 4311-9784.

Peaceful and cozy, walks and rural chores. Only with previous reservation.

❹ San Carlos
Just 2 km (1.2 mi) from Lobos. (east) Phone. (02227) 43-1351.

Colonial style building. Criollo and homemade dishes. Participation in the estancia rural chores.

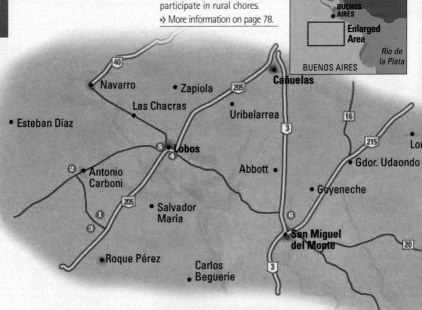

❶ La Concepción
Route 205, Lobos.
In Buenos Aires: Phone 4311-9784.

An elegant two stories mansion in French style surrounded by a magnificent park with lakes, fountains and statues. The visitor may ride horses, walk around the park, practice sports and participate in rural chores.

View of La Concepción

RURAL CHORES

Some of the estancias in the area offer tourists the possibility of engaging in rural chores such as milk cows, and manufacture of cheese, jam and other country products. Sometimes, it is possible to participate in farm labor.

TYPICAL DISHES. Estancias offer visitors a great variety of traditional and home-made dishes such as empanada, asado in spit and sweet pies.

SKILLS. Many establishments offer exhibitions of equestrian skills such as tame of a horse, races for a ringlet and special horse raced called *cuadreras*.

133

⑤ La Candelaria
Provincial Route 215, located 5 km (3 mi) from San Miguel del Monte. Phone. (011) 4313-3210.

One of the most famous estancias in the province, it offers lodging and different activities. More information on page 78.

⑦ La Mamaia
Route 20, located 16 km f (10 mi) rom Chascomús. Phone (02241) 42-4023.

An authentic estancia carrying out agricultural activities. The vi-sitor may ride horses, stroll around and enjoy traditional asados. More information on page 91.

⑧ La Horqueta
Located at the shore of Vitel Lagoon, Chascomús. Phone. (02241) 43-0646. In Buenos Aires: Phone 4812-7982 y 4813-1910.

The visitor may fish in the lake, sail in canoe and ride horses. More information on page 91.

⑨ Valle Santa Ana
RP 20, 6 km (3.7 mi) from Chascomús. Tel. (02241) 1568-6569.

Located near Chascomús, the visitor may ride horses or participate in rural chores.

⑩ La Fe
Provincial Route 20, located 30 km f (19 mi) rom Chascomús. Phone: (02241) 43-0290 Ext: 499.

Activities: horse riding and fishing. Located 140 km from Buenos Aires. More information on page 91.

Gándara
General Paz ⑦
⑧ ⑨
Chascomús
Don Cipriano
Cdte. Giribone
Adela
Monasterio
nueva

⑥ San Pablo
Provincial Route 215, located 5 km from San Miguel del Monte. Phone. (011) 4313-3210

With a spacious park, the visitor may ride horses, stroll around, practice sports and stay overnight.

La Mamaia.

Where to Eat

Many of the best Argentinian restaurants can be found in the outskirts of the city of Buenos Aires; along the river there are excellent freshwater fish restaurants while in the countryside around Buenos Aires you must try the traditional grilled beef. Also: a wide range of excellent Italian, Spanish and international restaurants.

ITINERARY 1

RESTAURANTS

Almacén El Tropezón
Paraná de las Palmas and Canal de la Serna, Tigre. Tel. 4728-1012. ⑤

Alpenhaus
*Arroyo Rama Negra, Tigre.
Tel. 4728-0422.* ⑤ ⑤

Boraso
*Arroyo Boraso, Tigre.
Tel. 4745-2594.* ⑤
International cuisine.

Carmela
*1810 Dardo Rocha, San Isidro.
Tel. 4717-2207. Open daily,
lunch and dinner.* ⑤ ⑤

TIPPING

In restaurants it is customary to leave a 10% tip for the waiter. Either leave it on the table or give it to the waiter.

Centro Náutico ACA Delta
*Situated on the left bank of the Luján river, where it meets the Benavidez canal, Tigre.
Tel. 4728-0407 / 10 / 12.* ⑤

Don Ramón
*412 Paseo Victorica, Tigre.
Tel. 4731-1322. Open daily,
lunch and dinner.* ⑤
Grill and international cuisine. Excellent buffet available, on the banks of the Luján river.

El Chapaleo
*868 Paseo Victorica, Tigre.
Tel. 4749-1901.
Daily, lunch and dinner.* ⑤
Grill and international cuisine.

El Gato Blanco
Río Capitán, Tigre. ⑤ ⑤
Tel. 4749-0655 y 4728-0390.

El Remanso
*Sarmiento River, Masmor Dock,
Tigre. Tel. 4728-0575.* ⑤
Interisleña boats get you here.

Fragata Hércules
*Isla Martín García.
Tel. para reservas 4749-0329 /
0931 / 2369.* ⑤

La Caballeriza
*1740 Dardo Rocha,
San Isidro. Tel. 4513-8888.
Daily, lunch and dinner.* ⑤

THE ASADO CRIOLLO RITUAL

There are many restaurants in all the towns in the region which serve traditional top-quality barbecues and grills. The most typical ways of grilling meat are the "Asado en cruz" method or grilling different cuts cooked with vegetables inside a metal disc.

PRICE RANGE

§ INEXPENSIVE

§ § MEDIUM-PRICED

§ § § EXPENSIVE

Both restaurants and bars exhibit prices on the menu on the widow-shop or outside the premises.

■ La Leonilda
802 Tiscornia Av. corner Pedro de Mendoza, San Isidro.
Tel. 4742-5371. Monday-Sunday, lunch and dinner. §
Situated opposite San Isidro station. Excellent grills.

■ La Riviera
Río Sarmiento, Tigre.
Tel. 4728-0177. §

■ La Vaca Atigrada
369 Lavalle, Tigre.
Tel. 4749-0698. Lunch and dinner. Grill room. §

■ María Luján
611 Paseo Victorica, Tigre.
Tel. 4731-9613 / 14. Tuesday-Sunday , lunch and dinner.
International cuisine. §

■ Molière
Canal Aliviador - Ruta 27, Tigre.
Tel. 4816-2507. § §

■ Pago de la Costa
1101 Primera Junta Av., San Isidro. Tel. 4743-2621.
Lunch and dinner.
Grills and international-cuisine. Includes duck pond and children's play area. § §

■ Paso del Toro
Río Capitán, Tigre.
Tel. 4728-0775. §

■ Posada del Abra
289 Arroyo Abra Vieja, Tigre.
Tel. 4728-0478. §
On the Interisleña ferryboat route (see page 125).

■ Siga La Vaca
2568 Dardo Rocha, San Isidro.Tel. 4717-1556 / 1298. Daily, lunch and dinner.
Grill room. §

≡ SPANISH CUISINE

Fish, seafood and olive oil are the key elements in Mediterranean cuisine. Paellas and rice with mussels (see photo) are two of the most popular Spanish dishes in Argentina.

135

■ Villa Hípica
222 Diego Carman, San Isidro.
Tel. 4763-5533.
Monday-Sunday, lunch and dinner. Friday-Saturday open till midnight. § §
Situated at San Isidro racetrack, it looks out onto the horse-breaking ring. Excellent Mediterranean cuisine, with fish as the specialty. Also has grill room.

ITINERARY 2

≡ RESTAURANTS ≡

■ 1800 Restaurant
Rivadavia corner Almte. Brown, Luján. Tel. (02323) 43-3080. § §
Steaks, pasta and fish.

■ Almacén de Ramos Generales
66 Bolívar, San Antonio de Areco. Tel. (02326) 45-6376.
Grill room. §

■ Dell 'Olmo
365 Alsina, San Antonio de Areco.
Tel. (02326) 45-2506. §

■ Don Pancho
Ruta 8 km 113, San Antonio de Areco. Tel. (02326) 45-6220.
Grill room. §

■ El Establo
Ruta 7 and N. S. de Luján Av., Luján. Tel. (02323) 43-0320.
Grill room. §

■ El Portugués
Ruta Panamericana km 49.5, Pilar. Tel. (02322) 47-2382. §

■ La Caballeriza
Ruta Panamericana km 50. Ramal Pilar.
Tel. (02322) 47-3082. § §
Monday-Sunday. Excellent grills, top-quality meat and a select wine list.

■ La Casona del Restaurador
Carlos Keen.
Tel. (02323) 42-9551. Grills. §

■ La Costa
Zerboni and Belgrano, San Antonio de Areco.
Tel. (02326) 45-2481.Grills. §

EMPANADAS TO SUIT ALL TASTES

Another traditional feature of Buenos Aires rural cuisine are empanadas (pies), especially with meat filling. They are either baked or fried, and are filled with minced or chopped meat with onion, peppers, olives and even raisins.

▌ La Perdiz
Route 6 and Río Luján, Open Door. Tel. (02323) 49-6669. ⑤⑤⑤
International cuisine.
Run by Paula de Felipe, in a marvelous setting. You must try the Pacific pink salmon.

▌ La Recova
Parque Ameghino, Luján. Tel. (02323) 42-2280. ⑤
Grill room.

▌ L'Eau Vive
2112 Constitución Av., Luján. Tel. (02323) 42-1774.
Tuesday -Saturday, lunch and dinner. Sunday: lunch only. Reserve in advance. ⑤⑤
Traditional European cuisine, French specialties. On weekdays they serve a dish representing the cuisine of all five continents. The waitresses are all nuns, and at Saturday and Sunday lunch, diners are given a rendition of "Ave Maria".

▌ Lo de Coty
Del Valle and Alvear, San Antonio de Areco. Tel. (02326) 45-27440. Grill room. ⑤

▌ Peña La Vieja Tortuga de Juan
60 Alsina, San Antonio de Areco. Tel. (02326) 45-6080. ⑤
Grill room.

▌ Puesto La Lechuza
188 Alsina, San Antonio de Areco. Tel. (02326) 45-5523. ⑤
Bar - Grill room.

▌ Rancho El Tata
Ruta 8 km 133, S. A. de Areco. Tel. (02325) 1565-8689. ⑤
Grill room.

▌ San Ceferino
Route 6 km 34.5, Open Door. Tel. (02323) 44-1500. ⑤⑤
This restaurant will only serve dishes to diners who book in advance its services.

▌ Siga La Vaca
Ruta Panamericana km 40.5, Pilar. Monday-Thursday: lunch. ⑤
Friday, Saturday and Sunday: dinner.
Grill room - buffet.

▌ Un Alto en la Huella
Belgrano and Zerboni, SanAntonio de Areco. Tel. (02326) 45-5095. ⑤
Traditional Grill room.

ITINERARY 3

≣ RESTAURANTS ≣

▌ Club de Pesca y Náutica
Costanera Av. and Lastra, Chascomús. Tel. (02241) 42-3231. ⑤
Situated on a small lake, freshwater fish is the restaurant's specialty, particularly the Pejerrey.

▌ Atalaya
Route 2 km 113.5 Chascomús Tel. (02241) 42-3212. ⑤

▌ De la Guardia
Costanera Av. and Corrientes, Chascomús. Tel. (02241) 42-4648
Lunch and dinner. ⑤⑤
Closed Monday and Tuesday.
International cuisine.
There are gardens in front of the building and the interior is decorated with beautiful lamps.

▌ El Náutico
Costanera Av. and Mitre, San Miguel del Monte. Tel. (02271) 42- 0607. Grill room. ⑤

▌ El Quincho
Route 3, km 111, San Miguel del Monte. Tel. (02271) 42-0208. ⑤

▌ La Casa de Mi Abuela
Salgado and Las Heras, Lobos. ⑤

▌ La Enramada
Ruta 3, km 110, San Miguel del Monte. Tel. (02271) 42-0653. ⑤

▌ Vieja Esquina
Costanera Av. and Artigas, Chascomús. Tel. (02241) 42-3733. ⑤

▌ Viejo Lobo de la Laguna
Dolores and Mitre, Chascomús. Tel. (02241) 43-6990. ⑤

THE DULCE DE LECHE

Different stories exist as to how it was invented, and in which part of the area around Buenos Aires.
In towns such as Chascomús and San Antonio de Areco they still make this delicious dish in the traditional way.

ITINERARY 4

RESTAURANTS

▌ **Abruzzese**
457 42 Street La Plata.
Tel. (0221) 483-0331. ⑤

▌ **Centro Basko**
14 corner 58 Streets. La Plata.
Tel. (0221) 451-7982. ⑤ ⑤

▌ **Crillon**
74 Diag. corner 8 Street La
Plata.Tel. (0221) 422-9089. ⑤

▌ **Don Clemente**
2651 44 Av. corner 148 St. La
Plata. Tel. (0221) 424-0980. ⑤

▌ **Dante**
41 St.corner 15 St. La Plata.
Tel. (0221) 424-9826. ⑤

▌ **El Argentino**
885 5 St. corner 50 St La Plata.
Tel. (0221) 427-2573. ⑤ ⑤

▌ **K'labaza**
68 St. between 24 and 25 St. La
Plata.Tel. (0221) 457-4698. ⑤ ⑤

TORTAS FRITAS

Tortas fritas (fritters) were traditionally eaten by country people to cheer themselves up on rainy days, and the tradition of eating them when it rains has been maintained. Buy them in stores and bakeries.

▌ **Imagina**
7 St. corner 53 St. La Plata.
Tel. (0221) 427-5747. ⑤

▌ **La Aguada**
631 50 Street La Plata.
Tel. (0221) 483-3163. ⑤

▌ **La Famiglia**
1566 74 Diag. La Plata.
Tel. (0221) 427-6141. ⑤

▌ **Mezzogiorno**
920 8 Street La Plata.
Tel. (0221) 483-3954. ⑤
CItalian cuisine.

▌ **Restaurante 1887**
6 St. corner 56 St. La Plata.
Tel. (0221) 425-7061. ⑤

▌ **Restaurante Propietarios de Caballos de Carrera**
146 80 Diag. La Plata.
Tel. (0221) 482-2301. ⑤ ⑤

ITALIAN CUISINE

The Mediterranean cuisine has become an important feature in Buenos Aires' gastronomy, and there are many top-quality Italian restaurants to choose from. Pasta is typically served with just garlic and olive oil (aglio e olio) or with sauces made using ingredients such as wine, basil, sun-dried tomatoes and cream.

Bagna cauda: a traditional dish from Piedmont.

137

FRESHWATER FISH

In the Tigre area and in the lakes of Chascomús, Monte and Lobos visitors can eat delicious freshwater fish such as Pejerrey and Loach.

Dishes made from Pejerrey.

Where to Have Fun

Outside the city limits there are lots of leisure and entertainment options available – fun parks, casinos and racetracks as well as a wide range of open-air activities such as horse riding and enjoying the local flora and fauna. There are also four zoological parks which are always popular with children.

THEME PARKS

There are several "educational farms" on the outskirts of the city of Buenos Aires: The Exploratorio is an interactive science center where adults and children can do experiments and have fun. The Parque de la Costa is a huge entertainment complex which has the largest " dancing water" fountain in South America, as well as lots of rides and shows.

Visitors can touch all the pieces on display at the Exploratorio.

Reaching the finishing line at a Sunday horse race.

■ **Parque de la Costa**
Estación Delta, Tren de la Costa. Tel. 4732-6300. Fr., Sat., Sun. and holidays. Open from 11 AM to 9 PM.

■ **Exploratorio**
1400 Roque Sáenz Peña, San Isidro. Tel. 4743-1177.

■ **Zoo Munchi's**
Ruta 25 and Panamericana, Escobar. Tel. (03488) 43-6600.

■ **Parque Roca**
3470 Roca Av., Buenos Aires. Tel. 4919-1542. Tuesday-Sunday. from 8:30 AM to 6:30 PM.

TIGRE CASINO

The Casino Trilenium complex in Tigre is 20,000 m² in size and has a wide variety of options: 8 restaurants, 7 bars, 70 gaming tables and over 1,500 slot machines, as well as spectacular live shows.

■ **Trilenium**
1385 Perú, Tigre. Tel. 4731-7000. Open Daily, from 11 AM to 4 PM.

HORSE RACES

There are two historical racetracks, at San Isidro and La Plata, where they also organize social events, and even auctions.

■ **Hipódromo de San Isidro**
504 Márquez Av., San Isidro. Tel. 4743-4010.

■ **Hipódromo de La Plata**
44 and 116 Streets, La Plata. Tel. (0221) 483-9994.

TROTTING RACES

Visitors can also see trotting races at the Hurlingham racetrack. To get there, take the Panamericana, then Rolón Av. followed by Roca Av. After you have crossed the railway line, the racetrack is only a few blocks away. Telephone: 4662-6363.

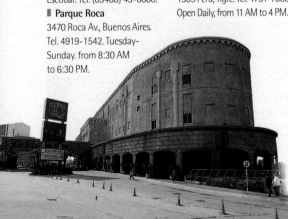

FACTS

WILDLIFE PARK
At the Estación de Cría de Animales Silvestres (ECAS) at La Plata, animals run loose in enclosures. Entrance only permitted by car.

SAN ISIDRO RACETRACK
148 hectares (370 acres) in size, it is one of the largest on the continent. The only Argentinian racetrack with a grass surface.

ZOOS

There are several zoological parks, the largest and most important of which can be found in La Plata and its surrounding area.

Elephant at La Plata zoo.

▐ Estación de Cría de Animales Silvestres (ECAS)
Camino Centenario km 16.200 Parque Pereyra Iraola, La Plata. Tel. (0221) 487-0920.

▐ Zoológico del Sur
800 Presidente Perón Av., Florencio Varela.
Tel. 4275-0614.

▐ Zooparque de Luján
Acceso Oeste km 58, Luján.
Tel. (02323) 45-5738 / 49-4218.

▐ Zoológico de La Plata
Paseo del Bosque w/n, La Plata. Tel. (0221) 427-3925.
More information on page 108.

HORSE RIDING

Horses can be hired for riding in the towns of Chascomús, San Antonio de Areco, Lobos and Moreno. Alternatively, you can take longer horse rides accompanied by a guide.

▐ Posta Los Rosales Cabalgatas
Demóstenes and Mendoza, Moreno. Tel. 15 4029-0245.

Birdwatching

The birders who visits Buenos Aires have a number of options to choose from: in the protected areas of the city and the surrounding area they can explore woodl and paths and pastureland and find over 300 species of birds.

BINOCULARS. *Birders often use binoculars of different ranges — 8x30, 7x50 or 10x50 — to get a better view..*

NOTEBOOKS. *It is useful to have a field notebook as well as an identification guide.*

RESERVAS
Ribera Norte
El Fomentista Av. (Camino de la Ribera) between López y Planes and Almafuerte. San Isidro. Phone 4747-6179.

Reserva Natural Otamendi
Route 9, Km. 80, Campana, Buenos Aires. Ph. (03489) 44-7505. Maintaining the river forest.

Reserva Natural Integral Punta Lara
Punta Lara, Ensenada. Phone (0221) 466-0396.

Reserva El Destino
Magdalena. Ph. 4803-9217.

Where to Shop

All kinds of traditional handicraft items are available, made from typical materials of the region. In the stores, markets and avenues you can buy leather products and fine quality traditional handcrafted pieces, as well as silverware and wood and cane furniture.

WHERE TO SHOP

Every area has its traditional products – San Antonio de Areco is the home of skilled silversmiths (the town is also famed for its traditional sweet specialties) while Tigre is renowned for its excellent wood and wicker furniture.

MADE TO MEASURE
The craftsmen in both Tigre and San Antonio de Areco will make pieces according to your measurements.

HANDICRAFTS

Traditional craft pieces are intermixed with rural imple-ments and horse-riding and polo outfits. There are many very beautiful, fine quality pieces on sale, made by famous traditional craftsmen.

❚ **Artesano A. Alvarez**
340 Alvear, San Antonio de Areco. Tel. (02326) 45-4219. Items in leather and silver.

❚ **Artesano José Rodríguez**
402 Guiraldes Av., San Antonio de Areco. Tel. (02326) 45-4741.

❚ **Tejidos en Telar Criollo y Pampa de Cristina Giordano**
112 Sarmiento, San Antonio de Areco. Tel. (02326) 45-2829.

❚ **Artesano Luis D'Ambrosio**
312 Arellano, San Antonio de Areco. Tel. (02326) 45-3745.

❚ **Artesano Roberto Falibene**
40 Belgrano, San Antonio de Areco. Tel. (02326) 45-3110. Ceramic pieces.

❚ **Artesano Raúl Marchi**
83 San Martín, San Antonio de Areco. Tel. (02326) 45-4345. Items in silver and animal horn.

❚ **Artesana Elba Iriarte**
261 Alsina, San Antonio de Areco. Tel. (02326) 45-2577.

RURAL ITEMS

The items of saddlery are internationally renowned, and include a wide range of traditional objects such as bolas, gourds, boots, wide-brimmed hats, bells, ponchos and traditional harnesses.

❚ **La Mansa**
128 Libres del Sur, Chascomús.

INDIAN HANDICRAFTS

Many stores sell traditional handcrafted items as well as pieces from indigenous cul-tures from all over Argentina. Some stores specialize in pieces made by Indians from different ethnic groups, par-ticularly the traditional masks of the Mataco-Chané people and their lignum vitae carv-ings. The black ceramics of the Tobas people and their neck-laces (made of beads, clay or seeds) are very highly prized. Of the different fabrics, pon-chos from Salta and natural wool stockings from Patago-nia are very popular. Many handcrafted items have cer-tificates of authenticity, which include the name of the craftsman and the technical data of the piece.

Silver neckerchief clasps.

▌ La Sillería
Muebles de Campo
75 Guido, San Antonio de
Areco. Tel. (02326) 45-4539.

▌ **Juan José Draghi**
345 Alvear, San Antonio de
Areco. Tel. (02326) 45-4219.

▌ **Oscar Lezcano**
Muebles de Campo
109 Alem, San Antonio de
Areco. Tel. (02326) 45-5523.

▌ **Calzado Criollo C. Fiore**
Arellano 266, San Antonio de
Areco. Tel. (02326) 45-2804.

≡ REGIONAL PRODUCTS ≡

In some areas around the city
of Buenos Aires, they make all
kinds of homemade foods and
items, including the traditional
dulce de leche (caramel spread),
fruit jams, honey, fabrics made
from plant fiber, candles and
many other handcrafted pieces.

▌ **La Olla de Cobre**
433 Matheu, San Antonio de
Areco. Tel. (02326) 45-3105.
Regional sweet specialities

Honey from hives
in Buenos Aires
province.

Dulce de leche
manufactured in a
handicapped people's
workshop in Chascomús.

▌ **Dulces Caseros Del Pago**
136 Emilio Zerboni,
San Antonio de Areco.
Tel. (02326) 45-4751.

▌ **Granja La Salamandra**
Ruta 192 kilómetro 12.5,
Exaltación de la Cruz.
Tel. (02323) 49-3335.

≡ SILVERWARE ≡

The handcrafted silver-
ware tradition dates back
to colonial days, and
there are many work-
shops with skilled
silversmiths. In San
Antonio de Areco you can watch
the craftsmen at work.

▌ **Taller de Platería Civil y Criolla**
250 Arellano, San Antonio de
Areco. Tel. (02325) 1568-0462.

▌ **Taller de Platería y Tal-abartería de Sergio Sánchez**
Alsina and Gral. Paz, San Antonio
de Areco. Tel. (02326) 45-5290.

▌ **Miguel y Martín Rigacci,**
Maestros Plateros
381 Belgrano, San Antonio de
Areco. Tel. (02326) 45-6049.

▌ **Taller de Miguel Bannon**
266 Arellano, San Antonio de
Areco. Tel. (02326) 45-5814.

▌ **Taller de Sergio Canali**
Ciriaco Díaz w/n, San Antonio
de Areco. Tel. (02326) 45-6265.

Basketwork stall in Tigre.

≡ WOOD AND WICKER ≡

In Puerto de Frutos in Tigre
and the surrounding area,
many stores specialize in fine-
quality furniture and furnish-
ings made from wood, wicker
and rattan cane.

▌ **Artesanías Llorente**
Loc. 4, Puerto de Frutos, Tigre.
Tel. 4749-0376.

▌ **Manos del Delta**
Loc. 162, Puerto de Frutos, Tigre.
Tel. 4731-4097.

▌ **Las cosas en madera**
Loc. 12, Puerto de Frutos, Tigre.
Tel. 4746-5330.

▌ **Mimbrería Any**
39 Las Casuarinas, Tigre.
Tel. 4731-4436.

▌ **Mimbrería Cicarelli**
6 Las Casuarinas, Tigre.
Tel. 4731-1435.

▌ **Manantial**
211 Las Casuarinas, Tigre.
Tel. 4764-3789.

141

COLONIAL JUG
You can find valuable silver pieces from the age of the Viceroyship in many stores and markets in Buenos Aires province.

TIE PIN AND SILVER CUFFLINKS
An attractive set of cufflinks and tie pin, with a classic design in the form of a small stirrup and a horse's head. Handmade Çin 900 silver, with an excellent finish.

POLO
Shirts, helmets, gaiters and polo mallets. Many stores in the area around Buenos Aires are famous for their high-quality articles. Polo players from all over the world buy their outfits here.

PAMPAS OUTFIT Pampas belts with thick black leather ends and a silver slide, made of 900 silver with gold inlays and with space for engraving a name or a monogram. Matching billfold.

LEATHER AND SILVER NECKLACE
A delicate necklace made of braided leather with silver features. The charm has a Fleur-de-lys pattern engraved in relief.

STIRRUPS
The Gauchos of Buenos Aires province only used stirrups for mounting their horses. In some specialist stores you can find stirrups made of iron, leather and strong leather.

MILK CHURN
An old iron milk churn, painted and patina-coated by hand. These churns were used by milkmen to deliver milk on their carts.

BOLAS
The traditional Gauchos' bolas were originally hunting weapons used by the Indians to catch deer and other animals.

MATE

Traditional dry gourd a variety of pumpkin) covered with braided leather thong. Silver maté-drinking tube.

EIGHT-THONG LASSO

Braided leather lasso. The lasso is one of the most important traditional implements for working on the plains. Eight-thong lassos are the strongest.

CHAMBERGO

The traditional hats of the Pampas region decorated with a hand-worked silver decoration.

143

PONCHO

A 19th Century poncho, manufactured in England from Argentinian wool. One of the most characteristic garments of the men of the Pampas, it consisted of a square woolen blanket with an opening in the middle for the head.

LEATHER DIARY COVER

This leather book cover decorated with exquisite embossed motifs can be used either for a diary or a notebook.

SADDLE

Fine quality saddle with Buenos Aires-style saddlecloth with asionera double matra, silk thread Pampa cushion and strong leather stirrups with silver rings.

SPURS

Iron spurs with "Nazarene" features a deriving from the sharp spur rosettes, which resemble the spikes on Christ's crown of thorns.

RIDING BOOTS

Long boots made from dark-brown buffalo hide. One of the many varieties of leather boots on sale in the saddlery stores in Buenos Aires.

ACKNOWLEDGEMENTS

Arandú
Aeroclub Fortín de Lobos
Alberto Julianelo (Museo Ciencias de La Plata)
Alejandro Bellefemine (Corporación Antiguo Puerto Madero)
Alfredo Llana (Dirección Gral. de Relaciones con Colectividades y Cultos GCBA)
Ana María Lang
Andrea Libson (Museo Nacional de Arte Decorativo)
Angel Oscar Prignano (Junta de Estudios Históricos de Flores)
Angela Corbalán
Antonio Mizerit and Miriam O´Black (Colectividad Eslovena)
Archivo Histórico de San Isidro
Arq. Adriana Herrero and Arq. Andrés Soudán (Arquitectura Teatral del Teatro Colón)
Arq. Alberto Boselli
Arq. Andrés Soudán
Arq. Beatriz Pérez and Diego Ruiz Museo Histórico Nacional
Arq. Elvira Buxadeira, Arq. Eduardo de Viarket and Arq. Rolando Alonso (Comisión Nacional de Museos y de Monumentos y Lugares Históricos)
Arq. Flora Manteola and Arq. Carlos Raspal
Arq. Graciela Raponi
Arq. Guillermo García and Arq. Martín Bai (Unidad Ejecutora Catedral de La Plata)
Arq. Jorge Hampton
Arq. Horacio Pando
Arq. Jorge Lestard
Arq. Jorge Tartarini, Arq. Celina Noya and Lic. Elisa Radovanovic (Museo del Patrimonio)
Arq. María Miyno (Biblioteca Nacional)
Arq. María Teresa Zagaseta (Centro Cultural Recoleta)
Arq. Mario Casares (Coordinador del Departamento Técnico de la Casa Rosada).
Arq. Marta Ibarborde (Centro de Investigación del Paisaje de FADU UBA)
Arq. Martín Gromez
Arq. Pablo Scannone
Arq. Pérez Ferrando
Arq. Ricardo Fernández Rojas
Arq. Rolando Schere
Arq. Silvia Terza
Arq. Susana Lago
Arq. Susana Mezquida
Arq. Arnaldo Pujal and Arq. Guillermo Frontera (Dirección Nacional de Arquitectura)
Arq. Leandro Lobosco, Daniela Shaio, María Laura Matta (Alvear Palace Hotel)
Carla M. Brunetti (Etoile Hotel)
Carlos Bottaro (Depto. de Obras del Club Boca Juniors)
Carlos Pallarols
Catalina Lentini (Subterráneos de Buenos Aires)
CEDIAP (Centro de Documentación de la Arquitectura Pública)
Comodoro Juan José Güiraldes
Correo Argentino
Cristina Farese de Monin (Museo Histórico de la Ciudad de Buenos Aires)
Daniel Baracali Costas (Jefe de Prensa del Teatro Colón).
Dr. Alvaro Ruiz Moreno (Subsecretario General de la Presidencia de la Nación)
Dr. Jorge Pelufo (Dirección Provincial de Islas de la Gobernación)
Dr. Eduardo Di Marco (Fundación Catedral)
Eduardo Prado (Bank Boston)
Elsa Talento (Basílica de San José de Flores)
Embajada de Arabia Saudí
Ernesto Mariano
Estudio de Arquitectura Mario Roberto Alvarez
Fotio Panaioti (Buque Museo Fragata Presidente Sarmiento)
Gabriela Camacho (Casa de la Pcia. de Buenos Aires)
Galerías Pacífico
Geraldo Preisz (Asociación de Descendientes de Alemanes del Volga)
Graciela Cacase and Andrea Clerici (Planetario)
Gregorio Plotnicki (Museo Manoblanca)
Gustavo Carrizo (Museo de Ciencias Naturales Bernardino Rivadavia)
Horacio Sanguinetti (Colegio Nacional de Buenos Aires)
Hugo Gigena and Arq. Hugo García (Palacio de la Legislatura de La Plata)
Ing. Juan José Briozzo (Catedral de San Isidro)
Instituto de Arte Americano Mario S. Buschiazzo (FADU UBA)
Jorge Alfonsin
Julio Alberto Hang (Jefe de la Casa Militar de la Presidencia de la Nación)
Lic. Fabián Falcó (Aguas Argentinas)
Lic. Eduardo Olivieri, Janine Wilson and Mercedes Rozenblat (Park Hyatt Hotel)
Lic. Julio Oscar Peyrano
Lic. Roberto Campbell
Lucía Sedon de Valery (Planetario)
Magdalena García (Biblioteca Sociedad Central de Arquitectos)
Manuel Güiraldes
María Angélica Vernet (Directora Museo del Cabildo)
María Paz Rodríguez (Relaciones Públicas del Hotel Alvear)
María Teresa Gaete and Néstor Paz (La Mansa, Chascomús)
Marta Magliano (Comisión Nacional de la Manzana de las Luces)
Matías Gigli and Jorge Aslan (Estudio de Arquitectura Aslan Ezcurra)
Mónica Kapusta (Jefa de Prensa de la Secretaría de Turismo de la Nación)
Morph
Museo de la Casa de Gobierno de la Nación
Museo de la Pasión Boquense
Museo del Patrimonio Histórico
Museo Nacional de Bellas Artes
Nora Tfchopp Podestá (Casa del Teatro)
Osvaldo Maza (Dirección General de Espacios Verdes del Jardín Botánico)
Padre Pucheta, Claudio Barú and Andrés Mage (Basílica de Luján)
Paulina Taiana
Profesor Antonio Cornejo (Director del Planetario)
Raúl Maggi (La Huella, Chascomús)
Rayo Rojo
Retro Toy´s
Sara Bianchi (Museo del Títere)
Saturnalia
Secretaría de Turismo de Chascomús
Silvia Bruzo and Arq. Leandro Villanueva (Obras y Mantenimiento de la Cámara de Diputados de la Nación)
Susana Lago (Centro Nacional de la Música)
Ulises Lencina, Marisa Miranda and Fabián Vinciguerra (Cámara de Diputados de la Nación)
Viviana Rivelli (Secretaría de Turismo de la Ciudad de Bs As)